Never Be Afraid To Walk The Path Alone

Mal Stevens

Never Be Afraid To Walk The Path Alone

52 Short-Stories of Inspiration, Courage, and Hope

Copyright © 2026 Mal Stevens

All rights reserved. No part of this book may be reproduced in any form or by any electronic or mechanical means, including information storage and retrieval systems, without prior written permission from the author, except by a reviewer who may quote brief passages in a review.

This is a work of fiction. Names, characters, places, and incidents are products of the author's imagination or are used fictitiously. Any resemblance to actual persons, living or dead, events, or locales is coincidental.

ISBN 978-0-6456803-7-9 (paperback)
ISBN 978-0-6456803-8-6 (ebook)

www.malstevens.com.au

Dedications

For **Marinda, Aimee, Steven, and Lily,** my daily reminder of all that is good in this world. I Love You X

~*~

Terry, Silla, & Scottie...sometimes the truest sign of support and strength is simply the quiet patience of letting someone arrive in their own time. I Love You X *mori non timeo*

suicide *noun*

/ˈsuː.ɪ.saɪd/

1. The act of intentionally causing one's own death.
2. *(figurative or philosophical)* When the pain of living becomes more difficult than the fear of dying.

Table of Contents

Dedications 3

mori non timeo 4

WHISPER TO THE READER 3

BIRAK 5

OBSERVATION 6

Week One 7

Week Two 11

Week Three 14

Week Four 17

Week Five 21

Week Six 24

Week Seven 27

Week Eight 32

Week Nine 35

Birak to Bunuru (Observation → Adaptation) 39

BUNURU 40

ADAPTATION 41

Week Ten 42

Week Eleven 46

Week Twelve 50

Week Thirteen 53

Week Fourteen 56

Week Fifteen 59

Week Sixteen 62

Week Seventeen 65

Bunuru to Djeran (Adaptation → Growth) 68

DJERAN 69

GROWTH 70

Week Eighteen 71

Week Nineteen 75

Week Twenty 79

Week Twenty-One 82

Week Twenty-Two 86

Week Twenty-Three 89

Week Twenty-Four 93

Week Twenty-Five 97

Week Twenty-Six 101

Djeran to Makuru (Growth → Resilience) 105

MAKURU 106

RESILIENCE 107

Week Twenty-Seven 108

Week Twenty-Eight 111

Week Twenty-Nine 114

Week Thirty 117

Week Thirty-One 121

Week Thirty-Two ... 124

Week Thirty-Three ... 128

Week Thirty-Four ... 131

Week Thirty-Five ... 135

Makuru to Djilba (Resilience → Connection) ... 138

DJILBA ... 139

CONNECTION ... 140

Week Thirty-Six ... 141

Week Thirty-Seven ... 146

Week Thirty-Eight ... 149

Week Thirty-Nine ... 153

Week Forty ... 157

Week Forty-One ... 161

Week Forty-Two ... 165

Week Forty-Three ... 169

Week Forty-Four ... 172

Djilba to Kambarang (Connection → Renewal) ... 175

KAMBARANG ... 176

RENEWAL ... 177

Week Forty-Five ... 178

Week Forty-Six ... 181

Week Forty-Seven ... 185

Week Forty-Eight ... 189

Week Forty-Nine 193

Week Fifty 196

Week Fifty-One 199

Week Fifty-Two 202

Author's Note - From My Heart to Yours 205

Acknowledgements 207

About The Author 208

An Excerpt from 'Light Codes: The Art of Stillness' 210

Preface 212

Introduction 214

Cosmic Overload & the Quiet Within 217

WHISPER TO THE READER

There is a wisdom written into the earth itself.

The Noongar people of Western Australia speak of six seasons, each carrying its own truth:

Birak (Observation), Bunuru (Adaptation), Djeran (Growth), Makuru (Resilience), Djilba (Connection), and Kambarang (Renewal).

Just as the land changes, so too do we.

Our lives move in seasons - times of fire and silence, of learning and letting go, of standing tall and beginning again. Each season whispers lessons, if only we choose to listen.

This book is a circle of fifty-two short-stories, one for each week of the year. They are stories of hardship and hope, of people who found courage where it seemed none remained, of light discovered in the darkest places. Each story invites you not only to read - but to observe, to pause, and to ponder what your own season is teaching you.

And so we begin in **Birak - The Season of Observation.**

For it is only when we learn to truly see - ourselves, the world, even the smallest butcher bird - that we begin to find the courage to walk the paths before us.

BIRAK

(December - January)
The hot, dry, pre-summer period…

OBSERVATION

A time of clarity and noticing changes in the environment, just as we reflect and observe as things shift and change in our own lives.

Introduction to Birak (Observation)

Birak is the season of observation, when the earth comes alive in its own quiet rhythm. It is a time to look closely - to see the small things that might otherwise go unnoticed, to observe life as it unfolds around us. In this season, we are invited to pay attention, not only to the world but to ourselves. In the moments of stillness, we discover the courage to walk our paths and trust the wisdom of our hearts.

Week One

Never Be Afraid to Walk the Path Alone…

Chloe had always been the kind of woman who blended quietly into the background. Life had not always been gentle with her. Her parents had passed when she was still quite young, her marriage had crumbled, and the few friends that she did have seemed to vanish the moment her life became the slightest bit heavy. She worked long shifts as a Nurse in a busy hospital, barely making ends meet, and went home nightly to an empty apartment that echoed with silence.

One winter evening, she found herself sitting on the park bench near her home, exhausted after another busy day at work. Around her, families hurried home together, friends laughed under shaded trees, and lovers leaned in close towards each other. Chloe felt invisible. Loneliness, once a quiet ache, now pressed on her chest so sharply she could barely breathe in the moment.

At that moment, something small caught her attention. A butcher bird, feathers ruffled by the cold, was perched on the fence. It was alone too - no flock, no warmth, no one to shield it. Yet the bird did not tremble. It hopped, it tilted its head to one side, and it sang a fragile but steady song long into dusk.

Chloe watched on, spellbound. 'Why am I so afraid of walking alone, when even this little creature dares to sing without company?' The thought was simple, but it shifted something deep inside of her. She realised she had been observing her life only through the lens of loss. That night, she decided to change her view.

Instead of fearing solitude, she began to treat it as a chance to discover herself. She started walking home the long way round through the park, observing the quiet resilience of trees that stood through storms, and the stubborn bloom of weeds pushing through concrete. She began writing in her journal - just small observations each day, like the kindness of a stranger who had held the door open for her, or the way the sunrise still managed to paint the sky gold even after the blackest of night.

Her perspective grew roots of strength. She enrolled in an evening class to learn a new language, she sat in a café alone sipping tea with her head held high, and she even travelled on a short trip up the north coast by herself. Each step she took taught her that courage wasn't the absence of fear – it was the willingness to keep moving even when no one walks beside you.

People began to notice a change in her. The once-quiet Chloe now carried herself with a quiet radiance, her smile steady and her words kind. She had no large circle of support, but she no longer needed one. Her courage became her companion, and her hope became her guide.

Years later, when she was asked how she managed through those hardest years, Chloe simply said, "Alone is not the same as lost. The path I feared was the one that actually shaped me. I stopped waiting for someone else to walk my path with me. I learned that the path itself was shaping me. Alone didn't mean abandoned - it meant free."

Reflection: Birak (Observation)

Birak is the season of watching closely - the crackle of fire on dry earth, the shifting of winds, the small signs that alert us that change is coming. It asks us to pay attention, not only to the world around us, but also to ourselves.

Chloe's story reminds us that even in solitude, there are lessons waiting to be observed: a butcher bird's song, a tree's patience, the way the morning sun returns without fail. These small truths are easy to overlook, yet they carry the quiet courage we need to keep moving forward.

This week, take a moment each day to observe one small thing that holds beauty, strength, or resilience. Write it down. Let it remind you that the path - whether walked alone or with others - is always teaching you something.

Sometimes courage is not in great leaps, but in noticing the little things that show us how to keep going.

Week Two

The Art of Seeing…

Philip opened his eyes and immediately thought he'd fallen in love.

It was right and natural that it should happen that way. Like many of his generation, he believed in the 'coup de rouses' - the lightning flash revelation between two souls, cutting through time and doubt.

"An angel," he murmured aloud, not caring who heard.

Eliza smiled softly as she dabbed a damp cloth across his brow. Her face, kissed by sun and framed by waves of auburn hair, seemed to glow in the soft amber light of the outback afternoon. She looked like the land itself - ancient, wild, kind. But it wasn't just her beauty that disarmed him. It was her quiet presence. Her stillness. The way she saw him.

Not the way others had.

Philip had fallen from his horse somewhere along the ridge of his family's cattle station - too stubborn to rest, too proud to admit he was exhausted. When Eliza had found him, he was bruised, broken, and worse - he was hollow. The years had worn him thin, but it wasn't the land that had done it. It had been the people in his life.

Lovers who had chipped away at him with doubt dressed as devotion. Words that lingered like ghosts. "You're not enough." "You're too much." "You should be more like this…" "Why don't you do that…"

Eliza didn't speak like that. She didn't try to fix him. She simply observed.

Day by day, as she nursed his body, she fed his spirit too - sometimes with stories, and sometimes with silence. She asked questions no one else had asked. She listened without flinching when his voice cracked. And slowly, Philip began to see what she saw.

That he was good. Kind. Worthy of loving.

One morning, as magpies sang in the trees above and sunlight slanted through the verandah posts, Philip turned to her and whispered, "You didn't just save my life. You reminded me it was worth saving."

Eliza smiled, brushing a curl from her face. "You just needed someone to see you."

And for the first time in a very long time, he believed it.

Reflection: Birak (Observation)

Birak teaches us to watch closely - not to judge, not to fix, but simply to see.

Philip's story reminds us that true healing often begins when someone observes us with kindness instead of criticism. To be seen clearly, without disguise or demand, is to be given permission to believe in our own worth again.

This week, try to look at someone in your life with the same gentleness Eliza offered Philip. See beyond their armour, beyond their weariness, and notice the quiet goodness in them. Sometimes, observation is the purest form of love.

To see someone is to help them remember who they are.

Week Three

Flip a Coin - Heads or Tails...

There are times in life when decisions weigh heavy. Do I stay or do I go? Do I take the risk or play it safe? Do I follow my head, or do I follow my heart?

Bridgid had always struggled with choices. She feared making the wrong move, feared the consequences of regret. And so, when faced with a decision that kept her awake night after night, she did what she had always done since she was a teenager: she flipped a coin.

Heads meant Yes. Tails meant No.

The coin spun high into the air, catching the light as it went, and clattered onto the table as it landed. Tails. The answer was No.

But instead of relief, Bridgid felt her stomach sink. A voice inside whispered: *That's not the answer I wanted.*

So she flipped again. "Best of three," she told herself. This time it landed on heads. She felt a flicker of excitement. She flipped once more, the coin tumbling in her palm, secretly hoping it would confirm what she already longed for.

When she finally stopped, the pattern was clear. She wasn't looking for permission from the coin - she was looking for confirmation of the choice her heart had already made.

Bridgid sat quietly, the coin glinting in the light. She realised the coin had never decided for her. Her own reaction had. The sinking, the soaring, the longing - they were her true answers.

From that moment on, she stopped fearing her choices so much. She began to observe the way her body, and her spirit, responded to possibilities. Did she feel heavy, or did she feel light? Did she shrink, or did she expand? Those observations became her compass.

The coin no longer held power over her. What mattered was the clarity that came when she dared to listen to herself.

Because deep down, we always know what we truly want.

The coin just helps us to see it.

Reflection: Birak (Observation)

Birak is the season of clarity - of sharp skies, watching fires burn, and noticing the signs around us. Observation teaches us that the answers we seek are often already within; we just need to pay attention.

Bridgid's story reminds us that indecision isn't about not knowing - it's about not trusting what we already know. The coin didn't give her an answer. Her own reaction did. The truth revealed itself the moment she observed her heart's response.

This week, when you face a decision, notice how your body and spirit react. Do you feel weighed down, or lifted? Tight, or free? Your reaction is the answer waiting to be seen.

Observation reveals that we often already know the answer - we only need to trust it.

Week Four

Life Moves in Seasons...

When Eleanor was six years old, her world cracked open for the first time.

It was a Friday when her grandfather passed — the only grandfather she had ever known. The house filled with hushed voices and unfamiliar stillness. Adults spoke in careful tones, and no one quite knew what to say to her. She only knew that someone important was gone.

That weekend passed in a blur.

On Monday morning, she returned to school carrying a sadness she didn't yet have words for. As she sat at her desk, the teacher announced that another girl's grandfather had passed over the weekend. Eleanor remembered looking across the room and thinking, *Friday it was my turn to be sad. Today, it's hers.*

She didn't realise it then, but that was her first lesson in how life works.

Everyone gets a turn.

As the years passed, Eleanor began to notice the pattern everywhere. One season brought laughter and ease, and another arrived heavy and uninvited. There were years of abundance and years of loss, moments of deep joy followed by stretches of uncertainty. None of it seemed fair — but none of it was personal either.

In her twenties, she sat around a table with friends, drinks in hand, talking about the lives they would begin once things settled down. Once the money was right. Once the timing was better. Once everything lined up.

But it never did — not all at once, and never for long.

That was the second lesson: you don't get everything at the same time. And if you do, it's only for a moment.

Life, Eleanor learned, is not stable by design. It moves. It shifts. It asks for constant adjustment. Relationships change. Bodies change. Fortunes rise and fall. Even the things we cling to most tightly eventually slip through our fingers, like mercury you cannot grasp.

Expecting life to be steady had only brought her heartbreak.

Understanding that life moves in cycles brought her peace.

Nothing that has form lasts forever. That doesn't make it cruel — it makes it real. Life isn't meant to be controlled or mastered or solved. It's meant to be experienced. All of it. The joy and the grief. The fullness and the emptiness. The seasons of holding on and the seasons of letting go.

That morning, as Eleanor sat at her kitchen table years later, the sun streamed through the window. Coffee was hot. Breakfast was simple and shared. Nothing extraordinary was happening — and yet, everything was.

Because today was a season of ease.

And she knew now how to honour it.

Reflection — Birak (Observation)

Birak teaches us to notice — not to judge, rush, or resist — but to see life clearly as it is.

This story reminds us that hardship and joy move in cycles. No season lasts forever, and none arrives as a punishment or a reward. Life is not singling us out; it is simply unfolding.

This week, notice what season you are in without trying to change it. Ask yourself: What is this moment teaching me to see?

Observation is the beginning of peace.

Life moves in cycles — and awareness softens every season.

Week Five

You're the Youngest You'll Ever Be…

Emma noticed it one morning while brushing her teeth.

The lines around her eyes hadn't appeared overnight — they'd arrived quietly, one smile at a time. She leaned closer to the mirror, not with judgment, but with curiosity. There was laughter etched there. There was grief, too. And strength she hadn't recognised while she was busy surviving.

She thought about how often she'd complained about getting older. About aching joints. About time moving too fast. About all the things she still hadn't done, and all the things she still had left to do.

Then the thought landed softly, like a truth she couldn't unsee: *I am the youngest I am ever going to be.*

Not tomorrow. Not next year. Today.

Emma thought of all the people she had loved who never made it to this age. Friends frozen in photographs. Names spoken gently, followed by silence. She realised how strange it was to resent something others had been denied. Age was not a punishment. It was proof.

That afternoon, instead of rushing through her day, Emma slowed down. She took her coffee outside. She noticed how warm the mug felt in her hands. She watched the way sunlight spilled across the grass. She laughed — properly laughed — at something small and ordinary.

Nothing dramatic happened. No great decision was made. No life was reinvented. But something shifted.

She stopped postponing joy for a "someday" that wasn't promised. She stopped measuring herself against past versions or future expectations. She let herself be exactly who she was — here, now, breathing.

Emma didn't suddenly love every part of aging. But she stopped begrudging it. Because growing older meant she was still here. Still learning. Still noticing.

And today — just today — was enough.

Reflection — Birak (Observation)

Birak invites us to notice — not just what is changing around us, but what is changing within us. Time passes quietly, whether we are paying attention or not.

This story reminds us that aging is not something to fear or resent. It is a privilege. Each year lived is evidence of resilience, experience, and survival.

This week, pause and notice one thing about yourself that exists because you have lived — wisdom, softness, courage, humour. Let it be something you honour, not something you rush past.

Sometimes the deepest gratitude begins with a simple realisation: You are still here.

Observation teaches us that growing older is not loss — it is proof that we lived.

Week Six

The Quiet Line Between Before and After...

Ethan used to think change arrived loudly.

With announcements. With certainty. With moments you could point to and say, *that was it — that was when everything shifted.*

But the truth didn't look like that at all.

It looked like a Tuesday morning.

The kettle boiling. The sun already hot through the window. His phone untouched on the bench.

Ethan stood there longer than necessary, noticing how still the house felt. Not empty — just quiet. He realised he had stopped rushing. Stopped rehearsing conversations that hadn't happened yet. Stopped carrying yesterday forward like a weight.

Nothing had happened exactly.

No breakthrough. No resolution. No miracle.

Just an awareness — subtle, almost easy to miss — that he was no longer standing where he once had.

There was a time when every decision felt urgent, reactive, driven by old habits and unexamined fear. He had lived as though life was something to keep up with, outrun, or fix.

But now, in this ordinary moment, Ethan noticed the line. The quiet line between before and after. It wasn't marked by achievement. It wasn't earned through suffering. It arrived through noticing.

He understood then that wisdom doesn't shout. It waits. It reveals itself only when you slow down enough to notice what has already shifted.

Observation isn't passive. It's brave. It takes courage to look at your life honestly — to admit what is no longer working, to recognise what keeps repeating, and to stop blaming the world for patterns you've outgrown.

Some people never pause long enough to see the truth. They stay busy. They stay distracted. They keep running in circles because stillness would force them to face what hurts.

But Ethan had lived through enough now to know this: If

you don't stop and look… you will keep choosing the same pain in different forms. So he poured his coffee, stepped outside, and let the day meet him where he was — not ahead, not behind. He didn't need the whole map. He only needed the next honest step. And for the first time in a long time… that felt like peace.

Just here.

Reflection — Birak (Observation)
Birak teaches us that transformation often happens quietly. Not all growth announces itself — some of the most important shifts are recognised only in hindsight.

This story reminds us that noticing is an act of wisdom. When we observe our own stillness, our softened reactions, and our changed pace, we realise we are already becoming someone new.

Change often happens the moment we finally notice it has already begun.

Week Seven

Everyone Gets A Turn…

Amy used to live like she was always late.

Late to become the person she thought she should be.

Late to fix what she thought was broken.

Late to catch up to the life everyone else seemed to be living with ease.

She didn't notice she was doing it at first. It just felt like motivation. Like ambition. Like "trying her best." But slowly, she realised she wasn't moving through life — she was *racing* through it. Always thinking about what was next, what was missing, what still needed improving. Even her joy came with pressure attached, as if happiness was something she had to earn through constant effort.

The lesson didn't come in a crisis. It came in a quiet moment that should have been ordinary.

One morning, Amy stood in her kitchen holding a cup of coffee she couldn't taste because her mind was already somewhere else. She was making mental lists, planning conversations, replaying old ones, preparing for problems that hadn't even arrived yet. Her body was standing still, but her thoughts were sprinting.

And then she noticed something. A bird on the fence line, completely unbothered by the world. The way the light hit the edge of the table. The sound of the kettle settling after it boiled. The softness of a simple moment she would normally bulldoze straight through.

It struck her, almost painfully, that she was missing her own life. Not because she didn't have enough to be grateful for — she did. But because she wasn't present enough to receive it.

That was the beginning of Amy's real wisdom: the understanding that life doesn't always change when you force it. Sometimes it changes when you finally see it.

She began to notice patterns — not in other people, but in herself.

She noticed how quickly she filled silence with noise.

How often she explained herself when she didn't need to.

How she kept proving her worth to people who had already

decided what they thought of her.

How she said yes out of fear, not love.

How she held on to things that were heavy simply because she'd carried them for so long.

And once she saw it clearly, she couldn't unsee it.

Amy realised something else too: observation isn't passive. It's powerful.

Because when you observe your life honestly, you stop living in reaction.

You stop repeating the same cycles, the same arguments, the same disappointments — not because you become perfect, but because you become aware.

And awareness is the first form of freedom.

She didn't wake up the next day magically calm. She still had habits. She still had old instincts. But now she had a pause — a tiny space between what she felt and what she did with it.

And in that space, she started choosing differently. She stopped chasing people who only loved her when she was useful. She stopped shrinking to keep peace. She stopped over-explaining her boundaries like they needed permission. She stopped treating rest like a reward and began treating it like respect.

And little by little, she became someone she trusted. Not because her life was suddenly easy… but because she was finally living it with her eyes open.

Amy learned that wisdom doesn't always arrive like lightning.

Sometimes it arrives like this: A quiet morning. A warm cup in your hands. A single moment where you realise you're allowed to stop running.

And from that moment on, she made a promise to herself: I will not miss my life while I'm busy trying to perfect it."

Reflection — Birak (Observation)

Birak teaches us to observe life as it is, not as we wish it to be.

This story reminds us that change is not personal — it is natural. Hard times do not mean we are failing, and good times are not rewards we must cling to in fear of losing them. Everything moves. Everything shifts.

This week, notice where you are in your own cycle — not to judge it, but to understand it. Peace comes not from control, but from acceptance.

Life is not meant to be held. It is meant to be lived.

Observation teaches us that change is not a flaw in life — it is life itself.

Week Eight

What Remains When You Stop Explaining Yourself...

For most of his life, Thomas explained himself.

Why he chose that path. Why he stayed. Why he left. Why he was quieter than before.

He carried his reasons like evidence, ready to present them whenever someone questioned his choices — or whenever he questioned himself.

But one day, without planning to, he stopped.

Not out of defiance. Not out of bitterness. Just... tiredness.

Tired of translating his inner world into words that never quite fit. Tired of defending decisions that already felt settled in his bones.

At first, the silence felt uncomfortable.

When people asked questions, he offered simple answers. When assumptions were made, he let them sit unanswered. He noticed the urge to clarify rise up — and pass.

What surprised him most was not how others reacted, but how he felt.

Lighter.

As if something he had been carrying for years had quietly loosened its grip.

Thomas realised that explanation had once been useful — a bridge while he was still unsure. But now, it had become unnecessary weight. Observation had replaced justification. Presence had replaced performance.

He wasn't hiding. He wasn't withdrawing. He was simply no longer narrating his life for an audience.

Birak teaches us this kind of seeing — that when we observe without needing approval, we begin to live more truthfully. Not louder. Just truer.

Thomas learned that peace often arrives when we stop trying to be understood and start trusting what we already know.

Reflection — Birak (Observation)

Birak invites us to observe where we expend unnecessary

energy. Sometimes growth is not about doing more — it is about releasing the need to explain what already feels right.

This story reminds us that clarity does not require consensus. When we stop over-explaining, we make room for quiet confidence and inner alignment.

Peace begins when explanation gives way to self-trust.

Week Nine

One Foot in Front of the Other…

Weekends didn't mean what they used to anymore.

Sundays used to smell like sausages on the barbecue and fresh coffee drifting through the yard. They sounded like talkback radio humming in the background, the soft clink of tools, the easy rhythm of two people pottering side by side. Now, weekends stretched long and hollow — filled with chores that never ended and a silence that lingered too loudly.

For a long time, Elodie moved through her days on autopilot.

Work. Home. Work again.

Gardening, cleaning, studying, surviving.

Always something that needed doing. Always just her now.

Some days, the question rose quietly inside her: *What's the point?*

One night, after a long shift, she said it out loud — not dramatically, not for sympathy — just honestly. "What's the point?"

She could be gone tomorrow. What difference did any of it make?

The answer didn't come from where she expected.

A colleague looked at her with steady calm and said, "You're doing better than you think. One day you'll look back at this time and realise how strong you were."

Later, her mother-in-law offered something even simpler: "The point is... chances are tomorrow you won't be gone."

It wasn't poetic. But it was true.

That truth stayed with Elodie.

She didn't suddenly feel hopeful. She didn't wake up healed or inspired. But the next morning, she put her feet on the floor anyway. She made a cup of tea. She stepped outside and noticed the air was cool. Noticed the birds arguing in the trees. Noticed that the sun still rose — whether she felt ready or not.

And slowly, something shifted.

She realised that survival doesn't always look brave. Sometimes, it looks like continuing.

Elodie stopped waiting to feel strong before moving forward. Strength, she learned, often arrives *after* action — not before it. Some days the only victory was getting through the day. Some days it was washing the dishes. Some days it was simply choosing not to give up.

And that was enough.

Because even when the tunnel felt long and the light distant, she was still walking. Still breathing. Still here.

One foot. Then the other.

That was all life was asking of her — and she was answering.

Reflection — Birak (Observation)

Birak teaches us to notice the smallest movements — the subtle ways we keep going even when everything feels heavy.

This story reminds us that progress is not always visible. Sometimes it is measured in breath, in routine, in the quiet courage of continuing when motivation has left the room.

This week, observe where you are still showing up — even imperfectly, even quietly. Let that be enough.

You don't need to see the whole path. You only need to take the next step.

Observation reminds us that survival itself is a form of courage.

Birak to Bunuru (Observation → Adaptation)

Transition:

From the sharp clarity of Birak, where we have learned to watch closely and notice the truths within and around us, we now step into Bunuru. Here, the heat presses hard and life asks us to adapt. Observation gives us awareness - but adaptation teaches us action. In this season, we learn to bend, adjust, and discover new ways to thrive when circumstances don't go as planned.

BUNURU

(February - March)

The hottest season, with little to no rain, where people traditionally moved closer to the coast for cooling breezes and seafood...

ADAPTATION

A time of adapting to changing conditions

Introduction to Bunuru (Adaptation)

Bunuru is the season of heat, when the land stretches, and we are tested by the challenges that life presents. It teaches us adaptation - the art of bending without breaking. This is a time to adjust, to evolve, and to find new ways to thrive. It is in this season that we learn resilience, embracing the changes and difficulties that come our way. Adaptation is not about avoiding the heat, but about learning to stand strong, even when life pushes us to our limits.

Week Ten

Letting Go...

The question came unexpectedly, the way the truest questions always do: *What is one word you would tell your younger self?*

The answer rose without effort.

Let go.

For years, Noah had believed that letting go meant failure. That releasing something meant he hadn't tried hard enough, loved deeply enough, or endured long enough. He held tightly — to people, to outcomes, and to versions of life that no longer fit — because holding on felt safer than the uncertainty of release.

But Bunuru has a way of teaching its lessons plainly.

The heat strips the land bare. Rivers recede. The earth does not beg the sky for rain — it adapts. Trees loosen their grip on leaves they cannot sustain. Clouds surrender what they carry. Survival, in this season, is not about force. It is about knowing what to release.

One summer afternoon beneath the vast Pilbara sky, Noah stood among others watching something drift upward — a bright balloon, vivid against the endless blue. It moved slowly at first, tugging gently, as though unsure whether it was allowed to go.

Then it was released.

No thunder. No drama. Just lift.

In that moment, something inside him softened. He realised that letting go was not an act of loss — it was an act of trust. Trust that what was meant for him would never require fear to hold it in place. Trust that what left his hands was never truly his to carry forward.

He thought of all the things he had been gripping too tightly: expectations that had grown heavy, stories that no longer told the truth, and relationships sustained by effort instead of ease.

And he understood — adaptation is not weakness. It is wisdom.

To let go is not to abandon hope. It is to make space for what can breathe.

That day, Noah stopped forcing answers. He stopped wrestling the future into shape. He loosened his grip — just enough — and felt something new enter the space he had been guarding so fiercely.

Relief.

Because what is meant for you will never lose you.

And what must leave does so to free your hands for what comes next.

Reflection – Bunuru (Adaptation)

Bunuru is the season of fierce heat — when the land teaches us that survival depends not on holding tighter, but on knowing when to release.

This story reminds us that letting go is not giving up. It is trusting the rhythm of life. When we loosen our grip on what no longer serves us — fear, control, expectation — we create space for clarity, movement, and renewal.

This week, notice where you may be holding on out of fear rather than truth. Ask yourself gently: What would happen if I let this go?

Sometimes courage is not found in holding on — but in trusting enough to release.

Adaptation begins the moment we loosen our grip and trust the path to carry what belongs to us.

Week Eleven

You Get What You Get, And You Don't Get Upset...

Three brothers grew up in a house where the rules were hard and simple: children were to be seen and not heard, and complaints were never tolerated. Their father had a saying he repeated like a drumbeat through their childhood: *"You get what you get, and you don't get upset."*

At first, the brothers tried to fight against it. Each one had dreams of their own - Tom wanted to study music, Daniel longed to play football, and Samuel dreamed of becoming a teacher. But in their strict household, dreams were luxuries. The choices were made for them, and when they dared to voice their own, they were silenced with the old phrase.

Time and again, they tried. Time and again, they were told no. Eventually, they stopped asking. By the time they were grown, "you get what you get" had burrowed into their bones. They took jobs they didn't want, stayed quiet in relationships that didn't nourish them, and accepted a life of settling.

But life, as it often does, had its own plan.

Tom, who never made it to music school, found himself repairing old guitars in his spare time. What started as a hobby turned into a workshop, and soon people came from miles around to have their instruments restored by him. His hands, denied the stage, still made music - just in another way.

Daniel, whose football dreams had been crushed, took a job as a youth worker. At first it felt like another compromise, but one day he found himself on a dusty oval, a group of boys begging him to kick the ball around. As he coached them, he realised his dream had not been lost - it had simply been rerouted. He was shaping players, not just playing himself.

Samuel, the quietest of the three, never became the classroom teacher he longed to be. Instead, he worked in a small library. At first it felt like failure. But as children came after school, eager for help with their reading, he discovered he was teaching after all - just not in the way he expected.

Each brother, in his own way, came to see that life had not denied them their dreams, but reshaped them. They hadn't gotten what they wanted, but they had gotten what they needed.

One evening, the three sat together on Tom's porch, talking as the sun sank low. Daniel laughed and said, "You know, Dad always told us, 'You get what you get, and you don't get upset.' Maybe he was half right. We didn't get what we wanted - but maybe what we got was better."

Samuel smiled, his eyes soft. "Maybe destiny knew the path before we did."

And for the first time, the old phrase no longer felt like a punishment. It felt like wisdom.

Reflection: Bunuru (Adaptation)

Bunuru is the season of fierce heat, when life presses against us and we must learn to bend, shift, and endure. Adaptation is the art of finding meaning even when things don't go the way we hoped.

The brothers' story shows us that sometimes not getting what we want is not failure, but redirection. Life has a way of shaping our paths in ways we could not have imagined. What feels like loss at first can become the very soil where our true calling grows.

This week, notice where disappointment may actually be an unopened gift. Ask yourself: What might life be giving me instead?

Adaptation is discovering that not getting what you want can become exactly what you need.

Week Twelve

Right Time, Right Choice…

For a long time, Ella believed that life happened *to* her.

Things didn't work out because of her childhood. She reacted the way she did because of other people. She stayed stuck because circumstances never quite lined up.

It wasn't that she was lazy or unkind — she worked hard, loved deeply, and tried her best. But whenever something went wrong, she could trace the reason outward. Someone else. Something else. Some unlucky timing.

"They say things happen at the right time," she would say quietly, half-hopeful, half-bitter. "I'm just waiting for mine."

But waiting became a habit. And habits, Ella slowly learned, can feel like safety while quietly stealing your power.

The shift didn't come with fireworks. No great awakening. Just a moment of uncomfortable honesty. One evening, after retelling the same story for the hundredth time, she stopped mid-sentence and felt it — the heaviness of her own excuses.

She realised something confronting, and that was that explanations can be true *and* still keep us stuck.

Yes, her past had shaped her. Yes, some wounds weren't her fault. But what she did next — how she responded — that part belonged to her.

Taking responsibility didn't mean blaming herself. It meant reclaiming choice.

Ella began to notice how often she reacted on autopilot — snapping, withdrawing, criticising, avoiding. She practised catching herself just before the words left her mouth. Sometimes she succeeded. Often, she didn't. But awareness was the first form of change.

It was uncomfortable work. Growth always is.

She learned that timing wasn't something life handed out like a reward — it was something shaped by readiness. By courage. By choosing to respond differently even when it felt unnatural or frightening.

Life didn't suddenly get easier. But it became lighter.

Because Ella was no longer waiting for the "right time."

She was meeting the moment she was already in.

And that, she discovered, was where her power had been all along.

Reflection – Bunuru (Adaptation)

Bunuru teaches us that adaptation begins with responsibility — not blame, not shame, but ownership. We may not control what happens to us, but we always have a say in how we respond.

Ella's story reminds us that while our past explains us, it does not define us. Growth begins when we stop handing our power to excuses and start choosing our responses with awareness and intention.

This week, notice where you might be waiting for life to change — and ask gently: What choice is already mine to make?

The right time isn't something we wait for — it's something we step into.

Week Thirteen

Work Hard – Quietly...

No one noticed Mark at first.

He arrived early, left late, and never made a fuss about either. While others spoke loudly about their plans, their hustle, their future success, Mark simply worked. Day after day. Same desk. Same tools. Same quiet focus.

He didn't post about it. Didn't announce milestones. Didn't wait for applause.

He had learned early that attention was loud, but progress was quiet.

Mark had once believed luck was something people were born with. That some lives simply unfolded more easily than others. But experience had taught him otherwise. The people who seemed "lucky" were rarely idle — they were consistent.

Every morning, he followed the same simple rituals. A walk while the world was still sleepy. Coffee in his hands. A few minutes of silence to steady his thoughts. He fed his mind carefully — choosing words, ideas, and intentions that strengthened rather than drained him.

There were days doubt crept in. Days when overthinking circled like a storm. But Mark had learned to notice it without letting it take the wheel. He reminded himself: action quiets fear. So, he moved. Even when unsure. Especially then.

He didn't wait for perfect conditions. He accepted imperfection as part of the process. If it mattered, he showed up — now, not someday.

Mark also learned to be selective with his energy. He didn't gossip. He didn't argue with critics. He smiled politely, listened briefly, and kept walking. His focus was forward, not sideways.

People sometimes mistook his calm for passivity. They didn't see the hunger underneath — the quiet fire that pushed him out of bed each morning. He believed he had something to give, something worth building, and that belief carried him through the long stretches where results were invisible.

Success, when it came, surprised others more than it surprised him.

Because Mark knew the truth they hadn't seen, that nothing about it was sudden.

It was built in small, unseen choices. In discipline over drama. In effort over explanation.

And most of all — in the decision to keep going, quietly, when no one was watching.

Reflection – Bunuru (Adaptation)

Bunuru teaches us that adaptation is often silent. Growth doesn't always announce itself — it unfolds through steady commitment, daily choices, and quiet perseverance.

Mark's story reminds us that luck is rarely accidental. It is shaped by action, consistency, curiosity, and humility. When we focus on the work rather than the noise, momentum begins to carry us forward.

This week, ask yourself: Where can I show up more quietly — and more consistently?

Progress is made quietly — consistency is its loudest proof.

Week Fourteen

Success...

For a long time, Grace thought success belonged to other people.

The loud ones. The confident ones. The ones who seemed to move through life without hesitation or doubt.

Grace had known struggle early. She had learned responsibility young, disappointment sooner than most, and resilience the hard way. While others chased applause, she learned how to endure. While others spoke about principles, she lived by them — even when it cost her.

Success, to Grace, never looked like trophies or titles.

It looked like getting up when it would have been easier to quit. It looked like walking away from people and places that dimmed her light. It looked like choosing integrity over approval — again and again.

She noticed something over the years.

The people she admired most weren't untouched by

hardship. They were shaped by it. They didn't compromise who they were when things became uncomfortable. Their character stayed intact when the pressure was on.

Grace began to understand that success wasn't about arriving somewhere — it was about how you travelled.

She stopped procrastinating on the life she wanted. Stopped waiting for permission. Stopped carrying resentment like luggage she never meant to keep. When anger surfaced, she acknowledged it — then released it. She refused to let old grudges claim permanent residence in her heart.

Her time, she realised, was sacred.

So she used it carefully. Loved fiercely. Acted decisively. Dreamed boldly — even when the dreams felt unrealistic.

She learned to walk alone when necessary, trusting that the right companions would meet her further along the road. She stopped using crutches — emotional, chemical, or relational — and strengthened her own spine instead.

Grace measured success differently now.

Not by money or recognition. But by the quiet pride she felt when she looked in the mirror. By the knowledge that her children were watching — and learning. By the certainty that when her life was done, she would have loved deeply, acted honestly, and helped where she could.

Success, she discovered, is not about being remembered for what you accumulated.

It is about being remembered for how you lived.

And Grace was finally at peace with the life she was building — one principled step at a time.

Reflection – Bunuru (Adaptation)

Bunuru reminds us that success is not forged in ease, but in adjustment. When life changes, we are asked to respond — not with denial, but with courage and clarity.

Grace's story shows us that real success is rooted in character. It is revealed in how we act when things are hard, how we treat others, and how faithfully we live our values.

This week, reflect on this question: What does success look like when no one is watching?

True success is living in alignment with your values — even when it costs you.

Week Fifteen

True Love…

There was a time when Nicola believed true love meant ease. That if something was meant to be, it would arrive without friction — effortless, intoxicating, wrapped in certainty.

And at first, it often did.

She fell for charm, for confidence, for the way someone made her feel alive in the beginning. The rose-coloured glow softened everything — habits, flaws, silences. What once felt like freedom later felt like distance. What once felt relaxed began to feel like avoidance. The very traits that had drawn her in slowly became the ones that hurt the most.

It took years — and more than one heartbreak — for Nicola to realise something quietly profound: We are often attracted to people not for who they are, but for who we hope they will become.

Across town, Daniel was learning the same lesson from the other side of the mirror. He had been loved for his potential more than his presence, admired for what he could be rather than accepted for what he was. When expectations replaced curiosity, love began to feel conditional.

Both of them, in different ways, were discovering the same truth: Love cannot survive projection.

True love doesn't ask us to become someone else. It doesn't require blindness, self-betrayal, or endurance disguised as loyalty. And it doesn't demand that we abandon ourselves to keep another close.

Bunuru teaches adaptation — not through self-erasure, but through awareness.

When Nicola finally turned her attention inward, she noticed something confronting: the qualities that irritated her most in others were often the ones she resisted in herself. The impatience. The fear of stagnation. The longing to be fully seen without fully revealing.

Adaptation, she learned, begins with honesty.

True love starts there too.

Not in fantasy — but in self-knowledge. Not in fixing another — but in meeting yourself clearly. Not in perfection — but in responsibility, compassion, and choice.

When love finally arrived again, it felt different. Quieter. Slower. Less dramatic — and far more real. It didn't promise forever. It offered presence. It didn't erase her edges. It respected them.

And for the first time, that was enough.

Reflection – Bunuru (Adaptation)

Bunuru reminds us that adaptation is not about changing who we are to be loved — but about growing into clarity.

True love asks us to see ourselves honestly, to release projection, and to choose relationships that honour reality over illusion. When we adapt in this way, love becomes a place of mutual respect rather than quiet compromise.

This week, reflect gently: Are you loving who someone is — or who you hope they might become?

True love begins when projection ends and self-honesty begins.

Week Sixteen

This I Believe…

Eleanor had reached the age where she no longer felt the need to convince anyone.

She had tried once — loudly, passionately, endlessly. She had argued her values, defended her softness, explained her ethics, justified her hopes. Over time, though, she learned something quieter and far more powerful: Belief does not need an audience.

What Eleanor believed lived in the small, unremarkable moments of her days.

She believed in choosing kindness when it was inconvenient. In teaching her children that integrity mattered more than applause. In pausing before reacting, even when anger rose quickly. In calling things by their true names — without cruelty, but without pretence.

She believed that children carried something sacred — a clarity adults too often lost. That they saw truth faster, felt injustice sharper, and loved without condition until taught otherwise.

She believed that distraction had become a substitute for meaning, and that stillness was not laziness but wisdom. That real work took time. That anything built too quickly collapsed just as fast.

Eleanor believed in honesty — even when it cost her. She had learned the hard way that lies, once invited in, multiplied quietly and poisoned everything they touched. So, she chose truth. Again, and again.

She believed in effort. In showing up tired. In doing the work even when no one was watching. She believed inspiration mattered — but discipline mattered more.

Some of her beliefs were gentle, even whimsical. She believed in rainbows. In wishing on stars. In the healing power of laughter shared at the right moment.

Others were forged through pain.

She believed that loneliness could be a teacher. That broken hearts could heal. That some souls had to wander longer before finding rest. That intuition was not imagination, but memory — carried forward from somewhere older than this life.

Eleanor did not claim certainty. She questioned often.

Changed her mind when growth demanded it. Adapted when life rearranged itself — as it always did.

What mattered was not being right. What mattered was being true.

In the end, Eleanor understood this: beliefs are not declarations. They are directions. And the truest ones are lived — quietly, imperfectly, daily.

Reflection – Bunuru (Adaptation)

Bunuru invites us to adapt not by abandoning our values, but by embodying them.

Belief is not something we announce — it is something we practice. As life changes, our beliefs may soften, deepen, or evolve, but they remain the compass that guides our choices.

This week, consider this gently: Are your beliefs something you defend — or something you live?

Belief is not what we say — it is what we choose, again and again.

Week Seventeen

The Weight No One Saw…

Everyone thought Hannah was fine.

She laughed easily. She showed up on time. She listened more than she spoke. If you asked how she was, she smiled and said, *"Good — busy, but good."* And most people accepted that answer gratefully, because it asked nothing more of them.

What they didn't see was how carefully that smile had been practised.

For years, Hannah carried her life like a sealed box — neat on the outside, heavy within. She believed that strength meant coping alone, that vulnerability was a liability, that asking for help would somehow confirm she wasn't enough.

So she adapted.

She learned how to function while unravelling. How to keep moving while her inner world collapsed quietly, piece by piece. She learned how to absorb pain without letting it show, how to sit at dinner tables and meetings while holding herself together by sheer will.

There were nights when the weight became unbearable. When the silence was louder than any noise, and the effort of simply existing felt immense. But morning always came, and Hannah always rose. She put one foot in front of the other and carried on — unseen, unsupported, unacknowledged.

The hardest part wasn't the pain itself.

It was the loneliness of it.

The realisation that suffering doesn't always announce itself — that some of the deepest battles are fought behind calm eyes and capable hands. That sometimes, survival looks like competence.

Eventually, something shifted. Not all at once. Not dramatically.

Hannah didn't suddenly "open up" or collapse into tears in public. She didn't find a magical solution or a perfect listener. What changed was smaller — and braver.

She stopped pretending she was fine to herself.

She began to acknowledge the truth of her experience. To name the exhaustion. To allow the pain its place without judgment. She learned that adaptation wasn't about denying what hurt — it was about learning how to live honestly with it.

And slowly, almost imperceptibly, the load became lighter.

Not because life became easier — but because she no longer carried it alone inside her own silence.

Reflection – Bunuru (Adaptation)

Bunuru teaches us that adaptation is not always visible.

Sometimes it looks like quiet endurance. Sometimes it looks like surviving in plain sight. But true adaptation begins when we stop performing strength and start honouring our truth.

This week, reflect gently: Where might you be telling the world you're fine — while asking nothing of yourself?

The hardest moments are often carried alone — until we allow ourselves to be honest about their weight.

Bunuru to Djeran (Adaptation → Growth)

Transition:

Adaptation has taught us how to shift and endure the heat of change, and now we move into the cooling winds of Djeran. This is the season of reflection and growth. Here, we pause and look inward, asking what lessons the struggles have left us with. Growth doesn't always arrive in leaps; often, it comes quietly, in the steady turning of the heart toward wisdom.

DJERAN

(April - May)

The beginning of cooler weather, with the environment becoming more settled…

GROWTH

A time of balance and growth in nature as people find their footing and develop.

Introduction to Djeran (Growth):

Djeran is the season of reflection and growth. As the earth cools and the winds begin to shift, we are invited to turn inward and examine what we've learned, what we've overcome, and where we are going. Growth doesn't always come in great leaps; sometimes it comes in small, steady steps.

Djeran teaches us that change is inevitable, but how we adapt to that change is what truly matters. In this season, we embrace the lessons that have shaped us and choose to grow into the next chapter of our lives.

Week Eighteen

Taking The Splinter from My Eye, and Not Seeing the Log in Your Own...

Some children grow up with laughter in their homes, safe places where they are encouraged to explore and be themselves. Others grow up feeling as though they are visitors from another world - aliens within their own families.

Lena was one of those children. From her earliest memories, she had been told to quiet her voice, to tame her imagination, to sit still and not question. Her parents, burdened by their own wounds and blindness, clipped her wings before she ever had the chance to stretch them. Whenever she reached for joy, their coldness smothered it. Whenever she tried to express herself, their disapproval silenced her.

The worst part was not the rules, but the absence. The absence of warmth, of encouragement, of being seen. Instead, there was only criticism, comparison, and distance. It left her carrying the sharp ache of never feeling enough. She grew into adulthood like someone always bracing for impact, whispering to herself, "Why can't they see me?"

For years, Lena carried that pain as proof that something was wrong with her. But one day, sitting in the stillness of her own thoughts, she heard a new whisper rise within her: "Hurt people hurt people."

It was simple, but it changed everything.

Her parents had not failed her because she was unworthy. They had failed her because they were broken themselves, trapped in patterns they had never healed. Their coldness was not a reflection of her value, but of their limits.

And so, she began the slow work of pulling out the splinters - all the sharp words, the moments of dismissal, the absence of tenderness. Each splinter hurt as she named it, but with everyone that she removed, she felt lighter. And as her eyes cleared, she saw that her parents carried whole logs of pain in their own vision. They could only love from the level of their own healing.

This did not excuse the hurt, but it explained it. It gave her space to grow past it.

Lena chose to stop defining herself by the wounds of others. Instead, she planted new roots - choosing friendships that celebrated her, building a home filled with warmth, and allowing her true self to breathe and shine.

She no longer wished for her parents to change. Instead, she wished for her own freedom.

And as she walked forward, she discovered something extraordinary: the very pain that had once convinced her she didn't belong became the soil for her growth. She had learned compassion. She had learned resilience. She had learned to see herself clearly, even when others never had.

Because sometimes, growth does not come from being nurtured. Sometimes, it comes from surviving what tried to diminish you - and choosing to rise anyway.

Reflection: Djeran (Growth)

Djeran is the season of cooling winds, of slowing down and looking inward. Growth often asks us to face what has hurt us, to see it clearly, and then to choose a different way forward.

Lena's story reminds us that people can only love and act from the level of their own healing. Hurt people hurt people. Recognising this truth does not erase the pain, but it gives us the freedom to stop carrying it as our own. In releasing what does not belong to us, we create space for our own growth.

This week, consider: what splinters of hurt are you still carrying that were never truly yours? Gently name them and then imagine laying them down. Growth begins in the small, brave choice to stop living by wounds and start living by your worth.

Growth begins when we stop carrying wounds that were never ours to hold.

Week Nineteen

Never Complain, Never Explain...

Brittany and Tiffany grew up in a household where silence was law. Their parents believed in the old saying that children should be seen and not heard, and they lived it with cold precision. Questions were ignored, opinions dismissed, laughter shushed. Their childhood was marked not by play or freedom, but by the careful art of staying invisible.

At school, the pattern continued. Without encouragement at home, the sisters shrank back in class, too afraid to speak up, too used to the feeling of being overlooked. Teachers assumed their quiet meant they had little to offer. Opportunities passed them by. Their confidence was smothered before it had the chance to bloom.

As young women, Brittany and Tiffany carried the invisible scars of that upbringing. They worked hard - harder than most - but always from a place of survival. They took whatever jobs they could find, never daring to imagine more. Their lives were defined by struggle, scraping by from one pay day to the next, haunted by a constant whisper: You don't deserve more. You're not enough.

It wasn't laziness. It wasn't lack of effort. It was the prison of belief that had been built for them long ago.

One night, after another exhausting shift, Tiffany broke the silence. "Why do we live like this?" she asked her sister. "We work harder than anyone, but it's like we're stuck in the same place."

Her question was the crack in the wall. For the first time, the sisters began to look inward. Slowly, painfully, they confronted the voices that had shaped them - the silence, the disapproval, the lessons that had told them to never reach higher. They realised that the biggest chains were not outside of them, but inside.

Together, they began the work. It was not easy. They read books about mindset, sought mentors, wrote down goals even when it felt foolish. They practiced speaking their truth aloud, even if their voices shook. They caught themselves when they slipped into thoughts of scarcity and replaced them with words of possibility.

And little by little, their lives began to shift. Brittany started a small business on the side, turning a hobby into income. Tiffany applied for a job she once thought was far beyond her reach - and got it. They stopped apologising for taking up space. They began to dream again, and this time, they dared to act.

For years, silence had been forced upon them. But now, they discovered a deeper truth: sometimes words aren't necessary. Sometimes the loudest statement you can make is to live the life you were told you could not have.

Actions speak louder than words. And Brittany and Tiffany's lives became a testimony - not only to the struggles they endured, but to the growth they chose.

Reflection: Djeran (Growth)

Djeran is the season of turning inward, of slowing winds and deep lessons. Growth often begins when we notice the silent beliefs that have shaped us and decide they no longer define who we are.

Brittany and Tiffany's story shows us that even when a childhood of silence tries to follow us into adulthood, we can choose a different way. Growth is not about erasing the past - it is about learning from it, changing our patterns, and allowing our actions to write a new story.

This week, ask yourself: What quiet belief from my past is still shaping me today? Notice it, challenge it, and then take one small action that speaks louder.

Growth is choosing to act beyond the limits of the past.

Week Twenty

What Luck Is Made Of…

People used to say Oliver was lucky.

They said it casually, almost dismissively, whenever something worked out for him. When his business slowly took shape. When his marriage stayed steady while others fell apart. When opportunities seemed to find him without fuss.

Oliver never corrected them. He just smiled.

What they didn't see was how early he woke each morning, before the noise of the world began. How he moved his body even when he didn't feel like it. How he fed his mind carefully, choosing words, music, and silence that strengthened rather than drained him.

They didn't see the people he quietly stopped spending time with — not because they were bad, but because they pulled him away from who he was trying to become. They didn't see the conversations he refused to engage in, the gossip he let fall flat, the criticism he didn't pick up and carry.

Oliver had learned early that luck wasn't loud.

It didn't announce itself online. It didn't boast or demand applause. It showed up in habits — repeated daily, often unnoticed.

When things went wrong — and they did — Oliver felt it deeply. He doubted. He overthought. He lay awake some nights wondering if he was fooling himself. But instead of letting his thoughts spiral unchecked, he learned to interrupt them. He chose movement over rumination. Action over paralysis.

He focused on the goal, not the plan. Plans changed. The goal did not.

Some days his progress looked messy. Zig-zagged. Uncertain. But he kept moving. One conversation. One decision. One small act of service at a time.

He remained curious. He asked questions. He listened more than he spoke.

He served others without keeping score. He admitted when he didn't know. He apologised quickly. He stayed grateful — not because life was easy, but because it was still a gift.

Oliver understood something most people missed: Luck isn't something you're born with. It's something you build. Quietly. Relentlessly. Imperfectly.

And when people called him lucky, he smiled — knowing the truth. Luck is what happens when you keep showing up long after no one is watching.

Reflection – Bunuru (Adaptation)

Bunuru teaches us how to live under pressure — how to adapt without burning out, and how to keep moving even when conditions are harsh.

Oliver's story reminds us that what the world often calls "luck" is usually the result of unseen choices: daily discipline, emotional restraint, self-awareness, and the courage to act before conditions feel perfect.

This week, notice what you are doing quietly, consistently, and without applause. These are the moments where adaptation becomes momentum.

Luck isn't chance — it's character practiced daily.

Luck is built quietly through daily choices — not discovered by accident.

Week Twenty-One

When Everything Falls Away...

There comes a moment in life when the dream you were living quietly collapses beneath your feet.

At forty-two, she had believed she was already standing inside the life she once wished for. She had chased her dreams with determination — if she imagined it, she built it, lived it, wore it like proof that happiness had arrived.

And yet, one morning, she woke with a hollow ache she could no longer ignore.

She felt empty. Stripped. As though everything she had worked toward had somehow dissolved, leaving her with nothing at all.

It frightened her at first — that vast, echoing space where certainty used to live. But then a friend said something so simple it cracked the heaviness wide open:

"Well, if you've got nothing... you're actually free to do anything."

The words landed softly yet shifted everything.

Because having nothing also meant having no walls left to hold her in place. No roles to protect. No version of herself to keep performing. In the emptiness, there was room — room for something new to enter.

She began to understand that breakdowns aren't always failures. Sometimes they are invitations.

An invitation to stop pretending. An invitation to change direction. An invitation to listen when life whispers, "This is not it."

Within that sentence lived another, quieter truth: "Yes... this is it."

She realised the greatest obstacle she faced wasn't her circumstances — it was her thinking. She had been measuring her life by what she lacked, rather than by what she could create. And in that moment, her focus shifted from resources to resourcefulness.

The energy of the breakdown still pulsed through her — heavy, raw, relentless. But energy is never good or bad. It is simply potential, waiting for direction.

Instead of sinking into worry, she redirected it. Instead of replaying fear, she chose curiosity. Instead of running from the discomfort, she allowed herself to feel it fully — and then asked better questions.

What do I want now? What no longer fits? What would make my life feel lighter?

She stopped filling her days with noise and distraction and gave herself permission to think. Long walks in nature replaced frantic to-do lists. Stillness replaced avoidance. And in that quiet, answers began to surface — not all at once, but enough to take the next step.

Some changes were small. Others were bold. But each action carried her closer to a life that felt aligned, intentional, and alive again.

The breakdown had not broken her. It had cleared her.

And in the space where everything fell away, something far more honest began to grow.

Reflection – Djeran (Growth)

Djeran is the season of reflection — the space between heat and storm, where growth begins quietly, from within. It reminds us that when life feels like it is falling apart, it may actually be making room.

This story teaches us that "this is not it" is not an ending — it is a doorway. When we allow ourselves to pause, feel, and re-evaluate, breakdowns can become breakthroughs shaped by intention rather than fear.

This week, ask yourself: What is no longer serving me — and what might be waiting to take its place?

Growth begins the moment we choose to see possibility where emptiness once lived.

"Growth begins when we stop resisting the breakdown and start listening to what it's clearing space for."

Week Twenty-Two

What I Learned Too Late...

Ziggy used to believe strength meant never backing down.

He pushed through exhaustion. Stayed too long in places that drained him. Said yes when his body and spirit were quietly saying no. He believed endurance was proof — proof to bosses, to partners, and to the world — that he was reliable, committed, and worthy.

It took becoming a father for him to see the cost.

One afternoon, whilst watching his son force himself through a race he clearly didn't enjoy, Ziggy felt a tightening in his chest. The boy ran with tears in his eyes, not because he wanted to finish, but because he thought he had to.

Ziggy didn't feel pride.

He felt recognition.

That night, he sat with his children and offered them something he had learned too late to receive himself.

"You don't earn your worth by suffering," he said. "Rest is not weakness. And walking away is sometimes the bravest thing you'll ever do."

In that moment, Ziggy understood what growth truly asks of us.

Not how much we can endure — but how honestly we can listen to ourselves once we know better.

Reflection — Djeran (Growth)

Djeran is the season of balance — the place between becoming and being. It teaches us that growth is not always about pushing harder, enduring longer, or proving ourselves through exhaustion. Sometimes, growth is learning when to stop.

This story reminds us that many of the lessons we wish we had learned earlier come not from failure, but from overextension. From staying too long. From mistaking resilience for self-sacrifice, and endurance for worth.

True growth asks us to listen — not only to the demands of the world, but to the quiet wisdom of our own limits. When we learn to rest without guilt, to walk away without shame, and to choose sustainability over struggle, we begin to model a healthier way forward for those who follow us. What we learn too late, we can still pass on.

And in doing so, growth continues — not through suffering, but through wisdom shared.

Wisdom is knowing when effort turns into harm.

Week Twenty-Three

Choose the Kindest Truth...

Rachel was careful with her words — not because she was timid, but because she understood their weight.

She had learned early that words could linger long after a moment had passed. That a sentence, once released, could echo in the mind for years. She knew this because she had grown up in a house where honesty came sharpened, and where truth was often delivered without gentleness.

"I'm just being real," people would say.

But reality, she learned, didn't need to bruise to be true.

Some of the deepest wounds of her childhood weren't caused by what was said — but by how it was said. Criticism masked as honesty. Harshness mistaken for strength. Silence used as punishment. She carried those lessons with her long into adulthood, watching how words could harden people, close hearts, and quietly erode trust.

When Rachel became a mother, she made a quiet decision.

Her children would learn a better way.

Not a softer truth — but a kinder one.

She began teaching them early, often in ordinary moments: at the kitchen bench, during car rides, in the aftermath of small disagreements. She taught them that honesty was not a weapon, and kindness was not a weakness.

"Truth without kindness is cruelty," she told them. "But kindness without truth is avoidance." "Growth lives where the two meet."

She showed them how to pause before speaking — to ask not only Is this true? but also Is this necessary? Is this kind? Is this the right time?

She taught them that boundaries could be firm without being cruel. That disappointment could be expressed without blame. That difficult conversations didn't have to end in damage if they were approached with care.

And just as importantly, she taught them how to speak to themselves.

Because Rachel had learned that the harshest words we hear are often the ones we repeat inside our own minds. She helped her children recognise when their inner voice became sharp, demanding, unforgiving — and showed them how to replace it with honesty that allowed room for grace.

Mistakes, she told them, are teachers — not verdicts.

As her children grew, Rachel watched something beautiful unfold. They learned to communicate clearly. To apologise without shame. To speak up without tearing others down. To choose words they didn't later wish they could take back.

Because words, once spoken, cannot be retrieved.

But they can be chosen.

And in choosing carefully, Rachel knew she had given her children something lasting — not just the ability to speak truth, but the wisdom to do so with compassion.

Reflection — Djeran (Growth)

Djeran is the season that teaches discernment — the delicate art of choosing wisely as we grow. It reminds us that maturity is not found in bluntness or silence, but in learning how to carry truth with care. Growth asks us to become aware of the impact of our words, not just their accuracy. What we say may be true, but how we say it determines whether it heals or harms, builds or erodes trust.

This story reminds us that kindness and truth are not opposites — they are partners. When we learn to speak honestly without cruelty, and gently without avoidance, we create relationships that can withstand discomfort without breaking. We also model something essential for those who learn from us: that strength does not need to wound, and clarity does not require hardness. In choosing the kindest truth, we choose growth — for ourselves, and for those who walk beside us.

Speak in a way your future self can stand behind.

Week Twenty-Four

Not Everything Is Yours to Carry...

Michael spent most of his life trying to fix everything.

He fixed problems before they were fully spoken. Smoothed tensions before they settled. Took responsibility for outcomes that were never his alone. He believed this was what it meant to be dependable — to be good, capable, and necessary.

If someone was unhappy, he assumed it was his fault. If something went wrong, he searched for what he could have done differently. If a relationship felt strained, he worked harder, gave more, and bent further.

For a long time, this made him seem strong.

But strength built on constant self-erasure comes at a cost.

Michael didn't notice how much he was carrying until his body and spirit began to resist. Exhaustion became normal. Resentment crept in quietly. He felt responsible for everyone — and deeply supported by no one.

The lesson didn't arrive in a crisis.

It arrived in a moment so ordinary it almost slipped past him.

One evening, he overheard his teenage daughter apologising — not for something she had done, but for someone else's reaction. Her shoulders were tight, her voice careful, already learning the art of making herself smaller to keep peace.

And suddenly, Michael saw himself.

He felt something inside him shift — not anger, but clarity.

He knelt beside her and said the words he had never been taught: "You can care without carrying." "You can love without absorbing." "What belongs to others is not yours to hold."

As he spoke, he realised he wasn't only teaching her — he was unlearning something himself.

Responsibility, he understood, had been confused with ownership. Compassion mistaken for self-sacrifice. Love tangled with obligation.

Michael began to notice how often he took on weight that

wasn't his — emotional weight, blame, expectations, outcomes. He had believed that if he didn't carry it, everything would fall apart.

But what actually happened when he began to set boundaries surprised him.

Relationships didn't break — they clarified. People didn't collapse — they stepped into their own responsibility. And the space he created by putting things down allowed him to breathe again.

Growth, Michael realised, isn't about becoming harder or more detached.

It's about becoming clearer.

Clear about where responsibility ends. Clear about what empathy does — and does not — require. Clear about the difference between support and self-abandonment.

By learning what not to carry, Michael discovered a quieter strength — one that allowed him to stay present without being consumed, loving without losing himself.

And that was the strength he wanted his children to inherit.

Reflection — Djeran (Growth)

Djeran is the season of discernment — the slow, thoughtful growth that comes from learning what truly belongs to us. It asks us to refine our sense of responsibility, to separate compassion from over-identification, and care from self-sacrifice.

This story reminds us that we are not meant to carry everything we feel. Growth does not require us to absorb the weight of others' emotions, choices, or outcomes. When we learn to set healthy boundaries, we honour both ourselves and those we love — allowing each person to stand in their own agency.

Putting something down does not mean we care less. It means we trust more — in others, in ourselves, and in the wisdom that knows what we were never meant to carry alone.

Growth begins when you put down what was never meant to be carried.

Week Twenty-Five

Do Not Rush Becoming...

Jasmine used to hurry everything.

Decisions were made quickly, before doubt could catch her. Healing was something to push through, not sit with. Forgiveness was offered before it had time to root. Even joy, when it arrived, felt like something she needed to grasp tightly before it slipped away.

She believed movement meant progress. That slowing down was a form of failure. That if she didn't keep going, she would be left behind.

Life, eventually, corrected her.

Not abruptly — but firmly.

Burnout arrived first, disguised as tiredness she couldn't sleep off. Then loss came, stripping away any illusion that effort alone could control outcomes. Grief followed, unresponsive to timelines or positive thinking. No matter how much she wanted to move on, her body and heart refused to rush.

For the first time, Jasmine had to stop.

And in that stillness, something unexpected happened.

She began to notice how much of her life had been lived in anticipation — always reaching for the next stage, the next version of herself, the next moment when things would finally make sense. She had been becoming without allowing herself to be.

As her children grew, she saw the same urgency beginning to form in them — the pressure to know, to decide, to succeed, to arrive. And she recognised it immediately.

This time, she chose to pass on a different lesson.

"You don't need to become all at once," she told them. "Growth is allowed to be slow."

She taught them that rushing does not make you brave. That patience is not weakness, but trust. That some lessons only reveal themselves when you stop forcing answers and allow experience to unfold.

She showed them that healing moves in layers, not lines. That forgiveness has its own timing. That clarity often arrives after confusion — not before it.

Most importantly, she taught them this: Becoming is not something to conquer. It is something to grow into.

Over time, Jasmine learned to measure progress differently. Not by speed, but by steadiness. Not by certainty, but by honesty. Not by how quickly she moved forward, but by how fully she stayed present where she was.

She discovered that slowing down did not shrink her life — it deepened it.

And in releasing the urgency to arrive, she finally allowed herself to become.

Reflection — Djeran (Growth)

Djeran is the season of steady growth — when change happens quietly beneath the surface, unseen but essential. It reminds us that development cannot be forced without consequence, and that wisdom often grows slower than ambition would like.

This story invites us to release the pressure to have it all figured out. Growth is not linear, nor is it urgent. When we stop rushing ourselves, we make space for understanding, resilience, and integration. What matures in its own time tends to last.

Becoming is not about speed. It is about alignment — with yourself, your values, and the season you are in.

Nothing meaningful grows under pressure alone.

Week Twenty-Six

Character Is What You Do When No One Is Watching...

Samuel was never one for speeches.

He didn't sit his children down to explain morality or list the rules of how to live well. He believed lessons landed deeper when they were lived, not announced. So instead of talking, he showed them — day after day, moment by moment.

They noticed how he treated people who had nothing to offer him. The way he spoke to the cashier who made a mistake. How he listened without interrupting. How he didn't change his tone depending on who was in the room.

They watched him admit when he was wrong — without defensiveness, without justification. No blaming circumstances. No rewriting the story to protect his pride. Just ownership.

They saw him keep his word even when it cost him time, money, or convenience. Even when no one would have known if he hadn't.

Especially then.

As they grew older, the children began to understand that their father was making choices most people never noticed — but always felt.

One evening, his son asked him a question that had clearly been forming for a while.

"Why do you always choose the harder path?"

Samuel didn't answer straight away. He thought for a moment, then said simply: "Because shortcuts shape character too — just not the kind you want."

He explained that reputation is something other people hold. It can change. It can be misread. It can disappear overnight.

But character — character is what you live with. It's the voice that speaks when the room is empty. It's the standard you carry when there's no applause, no consequence, no reward waiting on the other side.

Samuel taught them that integrity is not dramatic. It rarely draws attention. It is built in quiet decisions — returning the extra change, telling the uncomfortable truth, choosing not to take advantage simply because you could.

He reminded them that growth isn't proven by how loudly you stand for something when others are watching, but by how consistently you live it when they aren't.

Over time, his children realised something important: Their father wasn't trying to raise impressive people. He was trying to raise trustworthy ones.

And in doing so, he was still growing too — choosing, again and again, to be the kind of man he could respect when the day was done.

Reflection — Djeran (Growth)

Djeran reminds us that real growth happens beneath the surface. Before it is recognised, before it is rewarded, before it is seen by anyone else.

This story teaches us that character is shaped in moments without witnesses — in choices that offer no praise and no protection. Integrity is not about perfection, but about consistency. About choosing alignment between who we are and how we act, even when no one is keeping score.

Growth becomes sustainable when we stop performing for approval and start living by principle.

Character is built in the quiet moments.

Djeran to Makuru (Growth → Resilience)

Transition:

From the soft reflection of Djeran, we enter Makuru - a season of storms and testing. Growth has prepared us, but resilience is what carries us through the fiercest winds. Here, we learn that strength is not the absence of hardship, but the courage to rise again and again, even when the rains threaten to drown us.

MAKURU

(June - July)
The coldest and wettest season, characterised by storms, strong winds, and significant rainfall…

RESILIENCE

Enduring challenges and finding strength during the toughest of times.

Introduction to Makuru (Resilience):

Makuru is the season of cooling rains and strong winds, a time when the earth and its creatures are tested. It is a season that asks for resilience - the ability to endure through the toughest storms. This is when we learn that strength is not in the absence of hardship but in how we rise after every fall. The rains may come, but in the end, they nourish the land. Similarly, it is through our struggles that we find the nourishment of our deepest strength.

Week Twenty-Seven

Fixing Broken Legs...

There once was a beautiful young runner named Mollie who dreamed of crossing the finish line in a big race. Every morning, Mollie would lace up her shoes and try to run, but something always seemed to be holding her back. It wasn't a physical injury that anyone could see, it was something much deeper, a weight from something in her past that lingered deep within her heart.

One day, while struggling to push forward, Mollie met an older runner named Lonnie. Lonnie had noticed the hesitation in Mollie's stride and so asked her what was holding her back. After a moment of hesitation, Mollie shared that she felt weighed down by something, perhaps memories of a difficult situation during her childhood, or a time during her teenage years that had been full of challenges for her, and moments in time where she had felt trapped and she couldn't move forward.

Lonnie nodded knowingly and decided to share with Mollie a story of her own, a time when she, too, had felt unable to run because of invisible burdens of her own. Lonnie explained to Mollie that in healing the old wounds of her past that had kept her trapped and haunted her for almost a lifetime was like fixing a broken leg, you can't run freely so to speak, until you have taken the time to heal.

Over some time, with Lonnie's gentle guidance, support, and encouragement, Mollie began to confront each and every one of the memories as they surfaced, not to erase them, but to fully understand and accept them. Each day, Mollie felt herself become a little bit lighter, and a little bit stronger, until one morning, she realised that she was actually running the race without stumbling. The weight had lifted, and for the first time in a very long time, Mollie was finally ready to run her race.

And run her race she did.

As Mollie crossed the finish line, it wasn't just a victory in the race, it was a victory over everything that had once held her back. She had fixed her broken legs, and now she was ready to run the race, and she was running free.

Reflection: Makuru (Resilience)

Makuru is the season of deep winter - of heavy rains, strong winds, and long nights. It teaches us that resilience is not about never breaking, but about finding the courage to mend what has been fractured, and to rise stronger for it.

Mollie's story reminds us that healing takes time, and that unseen wounds can weigh as heavily as broken bones. But with patience, honesty, and support, even the deepest pain can be tended. And when it is, we discover that resilience is not just survival - it is the freedom to run forward, unburdened, into our own future.

This week, notice where you may still be carrying an old wound. Be gentle with yourself, and remember: resilience grows not from denying pain, but from tending it with care until you are ready to move again.

Resilience is not in never breaking, but in learning how to mend and run free again.

Week Twenty-Eight

Hello, Can Anybody Hear Me, Can Anybody See Me...

Once upon a time, there was a young woman named Lailey who always felt like she was living in the shadows. Growing up, Lailey often found herself sitting quietly at family gatherings, her voice drowned out by louder, more assertive relatives. In school, her ideas were often overlooked, even though she was full of creativity and insight. She would whisper to herself, "Hello, can anybody hear me?" hoping one day someone would truly listen.

As the years passed, Lailey discovered a passion for storytelling. She began writing down her thoughts and experiences, pouring her heart onto the pages. It was through writing that she found her voice, even if no one else had heard it yet.

One day, Lailey decided to share one of her stories at a local open mic night. Nervously, she stepped onto the stage and began to read. To her surprise, the audience was captivated. They listened intently, hanging on every word. For the first time, Lailey felt seen and heard.

Her story resonated with many people who had felt the same way she did. Lailey realised that by sharing her experiences, she could help others feel less alone. Her voice, once quiet and unheard, had become a source of inspiration and strength.

Lailey went on to write a book about her journey, and it became a beacon of hope for many who felt invisible. Through her courage and resilience, Lailey showed that everyone has a voice that deserves to be heard. And in finding her own, she helped others find theirs too.

Reflection: Makuru (Resilience)

There are seasons in life when we feel invisible, when our words echo unheard and our hearts ache for recognition. But Connection reminds us that every voice matters, and when we dare to share our truth, we not only heal ourselves - we light the way for others who have been waiting to feel seen too.

Lailey's story teaches us that courage begins in whispers but grows into something stronger the moment we offer it to the world. Our voice is not just for us - it can be the bridge that connects us to those who need it most.

This week, consider sharing a piece of your story with someone you trust. However small, your voice holds power, and in speaking it, you remind others that they are not alone.

Your voice is the thread that weaves connection - when you share it, others finally feel seen.

Week Twenty-Nine

Everyone Has a Cross to Bear...

There comes a quiet moment in grief when you realise something has shifted.

Not healed. Not finished. Just... different.

For Margaret, today felt like one of those moments.

For so long, she had told herself she was turning a corner — only to find the road folding back in on itself again. Grief doesn't move in straight lines. It loops, spirals, doubles back. And unless you have lived through the sudden loss of someone woven into the very fabric of your life, it is almost impossible to explain.

Margaret learned that grief has many faces.

At first, there was shock — a numb disbelief where reality felt unreal, where fear and confusion blurred together and her body moved through days on autopilot.

Then came anger — sharp and unpredictable. Frustration. Anxiety. Shame for feeling angry at all. Embarrassment at not being able to "hold it together" the way others expected.

Depression followed, heavy and suffocating. Energy disappeared. Motivation vanished. The world dulled. Some days, simply existing felt like more than enough.

And then — unexpectedly — came the need to talk. To reach out. To tell her story again and again, as if the words themselves might stitch meaning back into the wound. She bargained with life, searching desperately for why.

Over time, something softened.

Acceptance didn't arrive as peace — it arrived as space. Space to breathe. Space to imagine a future that looked different, but still possible. Space to consider that life could carry meaning again, even with the loss folded permanently into it.

Margaret realised something important: everyone carries a cross. Some are visible. Some are silent. Some reshape a person forever.

Grief had not destroyed her — it had stripped her down to what mattered. And in that stripping, she found something she hadn't expected yet: relief.

Not because the pain was gone — but because she no longer felt trapped inside it.

She wasn't "over it." She was moving with it.

And that, Margaret finally understood, was strength.

Reflection – Makuru (Resilience)

Makuru is the season of cold winds and heavy rain — a time that tests our endurance and asks us to keep standing when life feels relentless. Resilience is not about avoiding the storm; it is about learning how to live through it.

This story reminds us that grief does not follow rules or timelines. It comes in waves, cycles, and contradictions. But each time we survive another pass through the darkness, we build a deeper strength — one that carries compassion not only for ourselves, but for others walking unseen battles.

This week, remember: You do not need to carry your cross perfectly — only honestly.

Resilience is learning to carry what cannot be changed without letting it break you.

Week Thirty

Hurts Like Hell...

There was a time when Daniel believed that if you lived with integrity, life would meet you in kind.

He trusted instinct. He trusted good intentions. He believed that honesty would eventually lead to clarity — that lessons were meant to guide, not undo you.

He was wrong.

The hurt did not arrive all at once. It layered itself quietly — disappointment, misplaced hope, and relationships that did not become what he had believed they could be. Over time, the weight became difficult to separate into neat explanations. He could no longer point to a single moment and say: That was it.

He only knew that something in him felt worn.

What pained him most was not loss itself — but expectation. Daniel had believed he could help someone grow simply by loving them well. He had confused empathy with influence. He learned, slowly and painfully, that no one changes unless they choose to.

Compassion cannot substitute for accountability.

Letting go was not dramatic — it was sobering. He had to accept that some battles were never his to fight. That trying to rescue someone from themselves often costs you pieces of your own steadiness. In carrying what was not his, he had neglected what was.

And that hurt.

The turning point did not come through triumph. It came through fatherhood.

Daniel realised his children did not need perfection from him. They needed truth. They needed to see that pain is survivable. That boundaries are not cruelty. That walking away from what harms you is not weakness.

So he stopped pretending he was unaffected. He stopped chasing neat endings. Instead, he chose steadiness.

He allowed himself to feel the ache without dramatising it. To endure without hardening. To move forward without pretending it didn't matter.

He discovered something essential: Resilience is not about being untouched by pain. It is about remaining intact while you move through it.

The hurt did not disappear overnight. But it softened. Not because life became easier — but because Daniel stopped fighting what had already happened and began learning from it.

And in that quiet acceptance, strength returned.

Not loud. Not triumphant.

Just steady.

Reflection – Makuru (Resilience)

Makuru is the season of storms — when life strips us back and asks whether we will remain standing. Resilience is not found in denial or distraction, but in our willingness to feel deeply without abandoning ourselves.

Daniel's story reminds us that pain does not mean we have failed. Sometimes it means we are walking the hardest, most honest path forward. When the only way out is through, resilience becomes an act of courage.

If you are hurting, remember this: You do not need to be healed to keep going — you only need to stay. This week, ask yourself: Where am I trying to outrun pain that is asking to be understood?

Resilience is staying present with the pain long enough for it to transform.

Week Thirty-One

Be As The Tree...

There was a tree that had stood for longer than anyone could remember. Its roots reached deep into the earth, its branches stretched high into the sky, and its trunk bore the marks of years carved into its bark. Seasons came and went, yet the tree remained.

In summer, its leaves shimmered green and full, offering shade to children who played beneath it, books that were read in its quiet, and lovers who carved initials into its bark. Birds sang in its branches, built nests, and taught their young to fly.

In autumn, its golden leaves fell like confetti, covering the ground in a blanket that crunched beneath footsteps. Children laughed and tossed handfuls into the air, while the tree stood still, giving without complaint.

In winter, fierce winds battered its limbs, rains lashed its trunk, and lightning struck nearby. Yet the tree did not fall. It bent, it swayed, but its roots held strong.

In spring, blossoms returned, soft and fragrant, as though the tree had forgotten the storms that had tried to break it. New life always returned, again and again, as if to say: I will not be undone.

Over the years, people changed. The children grew up, the lovers drifted away, and some of the old friends who once sat beneath its shade never returned. Yet still, the tree remained - steadfast, patient, unyielding.

The tree became a silent witness to all of life's seasons: joy, sorrow, laughter, and loss. It did not turn away in storms, nor boast in sunshine. It simply stood, strong and unwavering, offering what it could without asking anything in return.

And those who passed by often found themselves pausing, resting a hand against its bark, and whispering, "If only I could be as steady as you."

The truth was simple: the tree's strength was not in never facing hardship, but in enduring it, rooted deeply, and rising again each time.

Be as the tree.

Reflection: Makuru (Resilience)

Makuru is the season of cold winds and heavy rains. It reminds us that resilience is not about avoiding the storm, but about finding the strength to stand through it.

The tree's story shows us that endurance is not a single act of bravery, but a lifetime of bending without breaking, of standing rooted when everything else shifts. Like the tree, we, too, can hold steady - offering shelter, presence, and quiet strength no matter what life brings.

This week, when challenges press hard against you, pause and remind yourself: storms may bend you, but they need not break you. Stand tall. Stay rooted. Endure.

Resilience is standing tall through every season, rooted yet unbroken.

Week Thirty-Two

Tears Flow Where Strength Is Forged

James had never been a man who cried easily.

He was known for keeping things moving — working, fixing, solving, and carrying on. When life demanded strength, he gave it. When others leaned, he steadied himself so they could. That was who he had always been.

Until grief found him.

Not all at once. Not dramatically. It arrived in quiet moments — driving alone, standing in the shower, staring at nothing in particular while the world carried on around him.

James had lost someone he loved deeply. The kind of loss that doesn't explode, but sinks. The kind that settles into the chest and stays there, heavy and unmoving. Time passed, but the ache did not lift. Friends assumed he was "doing okay" because he showed up, went to work, and answered questions with polite nods.

But at night, when the house was still, the tears came.

At first, he fought them. Told himself to pull it together. To be strong. To move on. He believed tears were a sign that he was failing the task of endurance.

He was wrong.

One evening, exhausted from holding everything in, James finally stopped resisting. He sat alone and let the tears fall — not in collapse, but in honesty. And something unexpected happened.

The weight shifted.

Not gone. Not healed. But loosened.

James began to understand that grief was not something to overcome — it was something to move through. The tears were not undoing him; they were carving space inside him. Teaching him how to carry loss without being crushed by it.

He noticed that on the days he allowed himself to feel, he stood a little steadier. On the days he suppressed it, everything felt heavier. Strength, he realised, was not forged by pretending the storm wasn't there — it was forged by standing in it, moment by moment.

James didn't become softer in a way that weakened him. He became quieter. Truer. More grounded.

He learned that resilience isn't loud. It doesn't announce itself. It forms in the places where tears are allowed to flow — and life is still lived anyway.

And so James kept going. Not because the sadness left, but because he learned he could walk with it.

That was where his strength was forged.

Reflection — Makuru (Resilience)

Makuru is the season of cold rains and long nights — a time when endurance is tested and strength is shaped beneath the surface.

James's story reminds us that resilience is not the absence of tears. It is the courage to let them come without letting them stop us from living. Grief does not make us weak — it teaches us how to stand honestly inside what cannot be changed.

This week, allow yourself to feel without judgment. Tears are not a failure of strength. They are often the place where true strength begins.

Strength is forged not by resisting grief, but by learning how to walk forward with it.

Week Thirty-Three

The First Thaw...

Clarissa learned resilience long before she had language for it.

She learned it in seasons where grief sat heavy in her chest, tightening her breath until even simple tasks felt monumental. She learned it in years where hope felt brittle — not gone, but fragile, as though one careless movement might shatter it entirely. There were mornings when getting out of bed was not an act of motivation, but defiance.

In those years, Clarissa believed strength meant pushing harder. Surviving colder. Enduring without complaint. Holding herself together at all costs.

She mistook numbness for fortitude and exhaustion for bravery. If she could just keep moving — just keep functioning — she thought she might outrun the ache that followed her everywhere.

But Makuru has a way of teaching its lessons slowly.

One winter morning, Clarissa stepped outside and noticed

something so subtle she almost missed it. The air was still sharp. The ground still cold. Frost still clung to the earth. And yet — beneath it all — there was movement.

Not warmth. Not relief. Just softening.

The frost hadn't disappeared. It had thinned.

That was when she understood something she had never been taught: resilience is not the absence of pain — it is the return of movement.

Healing did not arrive dramatically. It came quietly. As tolerance. As breath. As the ability to sit with discomfort without collapsing beneath it. As the slow loosening of fear around the future — not certainty, but possibility.

Clarissa realised that recovery often begins invisibly, beneath the surface, long before anything looks different on the outside. Long before others notice. Long before you feel ready to name it.

She stopped demanding that she feel better.

She stopped asking herself to be healed, hopeful, or whole.

She only asked herself to stay. To remain present. To keep breathing. To allow the season to pass in its own time.

And that, she learned, was enough.

Because even the hardest winters cannot stop the thaw.

They can only delay it.

Reflection — Makuru (Resilience)

Makuru reminds us that endurance does not mean remaining frozen. It asks us to withstand the cold without losing our capacity to soften again.

This story teaches us that resilience rarely announces itself. It arrives quietly — as patience when we want answers, as persistence when progress feels invisible, as trust that something beneath the surface is already shifting.

This week, remember, you do not need to feel warm to be healing. You only need to stay long enough for the ice to loosen.

Resilience begins the moment the ice loosens — not when it disappears.

Week Thirty-Four

The Weight He Learned to Set Down…

Cameron had always been the dependable one.

The fixer. The calm voice in a crisis. The man people turned to when things fell apart.

From a young age, he learned that being needed felt like purpose. So he became the one who stayed late, listened longer, absorbed more. He wore responsibility like armour, believing that if he carried enough, nothing else would break — not the family, not the workplace, not the people he loved.

But weight accumulates.

Years of holding others together began to settle into his body. His shoulders tightened. His jaw ached. Sleep no longer restored him — it merely paused the exhaustion. His patience thinned in ways he didn't recognise at first. His joy faded quietly, without drama or explanation.

Cameron told himself this was just adulthood. Just commitment. Just what strong people did.

Until one night, sitting alone in the stillness, he finally admitted the thought he had never allowed himself to finish: Some of the weight I'm carrying was never mine to hold.

Makuru has a way of stripping life back to essentials.

In the cold clarity of that season, Cameron began to see how often he stepped in before others had the chance to stand. How often he rescued instead of supported. How often he mistook over-functioning for love.

Resilience, he realised, is not about carrying more — it is about carrying wisely.

He began to practise small, uncomfortable changes. Saying no without explanation. Pausing instead of rushing to fix. Allowing others to experience the natural consequences of their choices — even when it made him uneasy.

This wasn't cruelty.

It was clarity.

And in the space created by setting some of the weight down, something unexpected happened.

His breath deepened. His posture changed. He felt taller — not because he was carrying more, but because he was finally standing in his own place.

Cameron learned that strength does not require self-erasure. That being supportive does not mean being consumed. And that sustainable resilience always includes boundaries.

The world did not fall apart when he stopped holding it up.

But he stopped collapsing under it.

Reflection — Makuru (Resilience)

Makuru teaches discernment — the quiet wisdom of knowing what must be endured, and what must be released.

This story reminds us that resilience is not measured by how much we carry, but by how long we can continue without breaking. Strength that ignores limits eventually becomes harm. Endurance that excludes boundaries leads to collapse.

This week, notice where you may be carrying weight that does not belong to you. Setting it down is not failure — it is survival.

Resilience grows when we stop carrying what was never ours.

Week Thirty-Five

What Stayed When Everything Else Left…

When Isla looked back over her life, what surprised her most was not what she had lost — but what had remained.

The things that she once believed would save her had not lasted. Certainty had dissolved. Plans had unravelled. Stability had shifted shape again and again. Jobs ended. Relationships changed or fell away. Roles she once identified with quietly expired.

Even the version of herself she had clung to — the one who believed life could be managed if she tried hard enough — no longer existed.

At first, this felt like failure.

Makuru has a way of making absence feel personal.

In the coldest seasons, Isla felt stripped back to something almost unrecognisable. Without the scaffolding of structure and certainty, she wondered who she was when nothing familiar remained to lean on. The quiet was confronting. The emptiness asked questions she hadn't been ready to answer.

But slowly, something else emerged. Not grand revelations. Not dramatic healing. Just clarity.

Beneath everything that had fallen away, certain things endured.

Her values — steady and intact. Her capacity to love — bruised, but not broken. Her willingness to begin again — even when she was afraid.

Makuru had taken much from her. But it had also removed what was never essential. In the absence of noise, Isla discovered that resilience does not live in what we accumulate or protect — it lives in what cannot be taken.

She learned to trust herself, not because life had become predictable, but because she had already survived unpredictability. She learned that endurance is not about becoming harder or more guarded — it is about returning, again and again, to what is true.

When the storms finally eased, Isla didn't rush to rebuild the same life she'd had before. She built a truer one.

One shaped by meaning rather than momentum. By alignment rather than expectation. By values that remained steady even when everything else shifted.

She no longer feared loss in the same way.

Because she now knew what stayed.

Reflection — Makuru (Resilience)

Makuru asks us to endure the stripping away — not as punishment, but as preparation.

This story reminds us that resilience is revealed when everything unnecessary falls away. When roles, structures, and identities dissolve, what remains becomes our foundation. Our values. Our integrity. Our capacity for compassion and renewal.

This week, reflect on what has endured through your hardest seasons. What stayed when everything else left may be exactly what you are meant to build upon.

True resilience is discovering what remains when everything else is gone.

Makuru to Djilba (Resilience → Connection)

Transition:

Having endured Makuru's rains, we now step into Djilba, the season of connection. Resilience has shown us how to stand firm alone, but Djilba reminds us we are never truly alone. Bonds of love, friendship, and shared humanity weave through this season, teaching us that the strongest roots are the ones that connect us to each other.

DJILBA

(August - September)

A transitional time with cooler air and the beginning of the floral explosion, marked by the blooming of the golden wattle...

CONNECTION

A transitional season marked by the first blooms and a kind of reawakening. A time when life starts to reconnect and flourish again like building relationships.

Introduction to Djilba (Connection)

Djilba is the season of connections - when the world around us is alive with relationships, with bonds that hold us together. In this season, we are reminded that we are never truly alone. Every connection, whether with family, friends, or even ourselves, is a thread in the tapestry of our lives.

Djilba teaches us that true connection goes beyond the physical. It is rooted in understanding, compassion, and shared energy. In this season, we embrace the power of human connection and the ties that bind us across time and space.

Week Thirty-Six

You Are My Sunshine, My Only Sunshine...

Michelle's life had always been measured in the rhythms of her children. Four sets of small hands that became larger ones, tiny shoes left at the door that grew into muddy boots, and laughter that once filled every room of her home. From morning until night, she had poured herself into motherhood - cooking, listening, cheering from the sidelines, drying tears, and tucking dreams into warm beds.

She loved them not as a group but as individuals, seeing each one clearly, Mollie with her fierce determination, Kittie with her gentle heart, Jesse with his endless curiosity, and Poppie with her mischievous grin. They were her sunrises and her sunsets, her reason to push forward even when life pressed hard. She lived and breathed them, every day, every moment.

But time is a thief, silent and certain. One by one, her children grew wings and flew into lives of their own. Michelle knew this day would come, but knowing didn't soften the hollow of the house when silence replaced laughter. Phone calls became quick. Visits became rare. Invitations dwindled as they moved into their own busy worlds of work, friends, and families.

She tried not to let it show. She smiled when they rushed off the phone with promises of "soon," nodded when visits ended too quickly, and whispered quietly to herself in the dark, *"You are my sunshine, my only sunshine."* But her heart ached with a loneliness she hadn't expected. She had given everything, and now the rooms she once filled with care stood still and empty.

One summer afternoon, Michelle found herself sitting on the back porch. The garden she once planted for the children's adventures bloomed without them. She felt the sting of tears until a thought came softly - love does not vanish when life moves on. Her children's lives, busy as they were, still carried the roots of everything she had ever given them. They might not come home as often, but she was still their sunshine, still the one who had lit their paths.

The next day, she decided to write each of them a letter. Not a letter to send asking for more time, or to guilt them, but silently as a reminder of a love that will never fade. She wrote of memories - of scraped knees she kissed, of songs sung in the kitchen, of the dreams she still held for them. She ended each letter with the same words: *"No matter where you are in this big, wide world, you are my Sunshine. And I am always here, loving you."*

Michelle tucked the letters away in a small wooden box by her bedside. They would never be sent, never answered, but that didn't matter. They were her way of keeping her children close, of holding them in the only way she still could.

Her house remained quiet. The phone rang less often than she wished. Yet in the quiet, Michelle carried on. She hummed their song while watering the garden, whispered it into the folds of laundry, and let it echo softly through the empty rooms.

For though her children were far away, they were still her sunshine. Her only sunshine. And she would love them, fiercely and forever, even from the shadows of silence.

Reflection: Djilba (Connection)

Djilba is the season of families - of nurturing and giving, of holding close what we love most. But Connection also reminds us that love is not always returned in the way we long for. Sometimes it is carried quietly, unspoken, unseen - yet still strong and unbreakable.

Michelle's story shows us that even in the ache of absence, love endures. The roots we have planted remain, even when the branches stretch far from us. Connection does not fade because of distance; it is kept alive by the love we continue to hold, even when no one else sees it.

This week, if you feel unseen or left behind by those you love, remember: your love is still a light. Even if no one pauses to notice, it still shines, and it still matters.

Love endures, even when carried quietly and unseen.

Week Thirty-Seven

Affinity Friends…

When Ebony first met Teddie, she would have struggled to explain why their connection felt so immediate.

They worked in the same place, crossed paths in hallways, shared polite conversations over cups of tea. On the surface, they were two very different women. Their lives had unfolded along separate roads — shaped by different histories, different losses, and different lessons learned the hard way.

And yet, from the beginning, something about Teddie felt familiar.

Ebony noticed it in small ways. The way Teddie listened without interrupting. The way she spoke honestly, even when it would have been easier to stay quiet. The way kindness seemed to guide her choices, not as an act, but as a value she lived by.

Ebony found herself looking forward to the days Teddie was there. Conversations came easily. Silences felt comfortable. There was no need to explain herself or soften her edges. She could simply be.

It made Ebony wonder why some people drift into our lives without effort, while others — no matter how hard we try — never quite fit.

She came across a line by Frank L. Hammer that finally gave words to what she was feeling: *"Affinity is the mind's law of attraction, and we gravitate to where we belong. Like attracts like… The mind is a magnet and draws to itself all things of like nature."*

The realisation settled gently.

Ebony hadn't attracted Teddie by accident. She had drawn her in by becoming more herself — by choosing honesty over approval, integrity over convenience, kindness over fear. Teddie simply reflected those same qualities back to her.

What looked "unlikely" to others made perfect sense to Ebony. This friendship wasn't built on similarity of circumstance, but on resonance of values.

Teddie was her affinity friend.

And in recognising that, Ebony felt something deeper than gratitude for the friendship itself. She felt proud — not just of the connection, but of who she had become to invite it into her life.

Reflection – Djilba (Connection)

Djilba is the season of connection — when life weaves itself back together through relationships, shared warmth, and unseen bonds. It reminds us that true connection does not arrive through effort or chance, but through alignment.

This story teaches us that affinity is not random. When we live in truth, kindness, and integrity, we naturally draw people who recognise those same qualities within themselves.

This week, notice who you are drawn to and why. It may say as much about you as it does about them.

True connection is born of affinity - we attract what we are ready to receive.

Week Thirty-Eight

Where There Is Love, There Is No Death...

Clara met Henry when she was eighteen and still believed life unfolded in straight lines.

She had dreamed of studying nursing, of caring for others with her hands and her heart, but those dreams were quietly folded away by voices that told her love should come first — that ambition could wait. So she worked as a secretary instead, telling herself it was only temporary.

Henry was nineteen when she met him. He had an easy kindness about him, the kind that didn't try to impress. He listened more than he spoke. He noticed things others missed. Their connection was immediate, unforced — as if two pieces of a story had finally found their place beside one another.

They built a life quickly, but not recklessly. Four children followed. Four small lives woven into theirs. The house was loud, busy, imperfect — and full. Exhaustion lived alongside joy. Love showed up in ordinary moments: packed lunches, late nights, and shared glances across crowded rooms.

Then one ordinary day fractured everything.

A motor vehicle accident took Henry without warning. Clara was forty when she became a widow — a word that felt far too heavy for her body to carry.

Twelve years have passed since that day, yet grief has never obeyed the calendar. Clara still misses him with a sharpness that surprises her. Some nights the silence presses in so tightly she feels it in her chest. People ask her gently, Do you think you'll see him again?

Her answer has never wavered. Yes. Because love, she has learned, does not end.

Here on earth, love looks like shared lives and shared burdens. In the deeper realms — whatever name we give them — love is law. Souls bound by genuine love do not lose one another. Bodies separate. Love does not.

Clara believes Henry is still moving toward her, just as she is moving toward him — not impatiently, not desperately, but inevitably. The same force that once drew them together continues its quiet work.

Until then, she lives.

She walks forward for their children. She gives kindness where she can. She pours love into the world because she trusts that love shapes what comes next. Grief has not made her smaller — it has made her truer.

The ache remains. It always will. But it no longer feels like an ending.

It feels like a continuation.

Because death, Clara understands now, did not take Henry from her.

It only changed the distance.

Reflection — Djilba (Connection)

Djilba reminds us that connection does not end when form changes. Love is not confined to presence, proximity, or even time. It is the deepest thread we carry — one that continues to bind us through absence and loss.

Clara's story teaches us that grief and love are not opposites. They coexist. And when love is real, it is not erased by death — it is transformed.

This week, if you are missing someone who shaped your life, remember this: Love does not disappear. It continues — quietly, faithfully — until it finds you again.

Connection teaches us that where there is love, there is no death.

Week Thirty-Nine

More Than Meets the Eye...

Grace had been a Registered Nurse for just over three years when she learned a quiet truth that no textbook had ever taught her: that most people only ever see the surface.

They see the calm voice. The steady hands. The woman standing at the bedside who seems to know what to do next.

They do not see what lives underneath.

On one long shift in critical care, Grace was caring for a very sick man. His recovery was complicated, his body tethered to machines, medications adjusted minute by minute. Tubes and wires traced across his chest, and the room pulsed with alarms that sliced through the silence like sudden fear.

His wife stood close. Watching everything. Hoping. Breaking.

Grace had spoken with her many times over the past two days — explaining gently, honestly, never promising more than she could give. When another alarm sounded and Grace moved quickly to stabilise the situation, she tried to offer reassurance.

"It's okay," she said softly. "We see this often. We're used to managing it."

The words landed wrong.

The woman turned on her, grief sharpened into anger. "How would you feel if it was your husband in that bed?" she cried. "You have no idea. You'd be worried too."

Grace felt it then — the familiar ache rising in her chest.

She apologised. She stepped back. She gave the woman space.

What she did not say were the words echoing loudly inside her: I do know how you feel. I wish it were my husband in that bed.

But Grace had learned that some truths must remain unspoken.

She had learned to wear calm like a uniform. To move efficiently even when chaos erupted. To stay steady while others fell apart. People might see her composed while tears fell around her, or laughing quietly later in the corridor.

They would not see the grief beneath the smile.

They would not know that when she watched a wife hold her husband's hand, her own loss stirred — reopened like a wound that never quite healed. They would not know that her steadiness was not indifference, but discipline. If she allowed the feelings to spill freely, she feared she might not gather them back again in time to do what needed to be done.

So instead of tears, they saw competence. Instead of sorrow, they saw presence.

Over time, Grace came to understand something deeper: nurses carry their own histories into every room. Loss. Addiction. Trauma. Illness. Heartbreak. Stories rarely spoken aloud. Many have stood exactly where families now stand — terrified, helpless, praying for outcomes they cannot control.

They do not judge.

They remember.

Grace realised that her strength was not the absence of pain

— it was the ability to hold her own pain quietly while helping someone else hold theirs.

That was the wisdom nursing gave her.

And so now, when she stands at a bedside, she knows this: there is always more happening than what can be seen.

The nurse is not untouched by suffering. She is standing beside it — carrying her own story with grace.

Reflection – Djilba (Connection)

Djilba is the season of connection — the quiet, unseen bonds that form when hearts recognise one another without words. It reminds us that empathy often flows silently, carried in presence rather than speech.

This story teaches us that those who care for us are not untouched by pain — they are often deeply familiar with it. And it is precisely this understanding that allows them to hold space for others with such grace.

This week, remember: The deepest connections are often the ones we never see.

True connection lives beneath the surface — in the quiet understanding we carry for one another.

Week Forty

Who Walked With Me...

Maeve used to believe independence meant not needing anyone.

She had learned early how to rely on herself — how to manage, organise, endure. She was capable, efficient, self-contained. If she carried her own weight, if she handled her own storms quietly, then no one could disappoint her or leave her stranded in the aftermath.

Independence felt like safety.

For a long time, it worked.

Until it didn't.

Life didn't shatter all at once. It wore her down instead — through grief that arrived without warning, exhaustion that sleep could not touch, and responsibilities that stacked quietly until her breath felt shallow. There was no dramatic collapse. Just a slow unravelling of the belief that she could hold everything alone.

And when the cracks widened, it wasn't her strength that saved her.

It was the people she hadn't realised she was still letting in.

A friend who arrived with groceries and no questions. A sister who sat beside her, saying nothing, doing nothing — but leaving the door open to tears. A neighbour who checked in weeks later, when everyone else had returned to their own lives.

None of them fixed anything. None of them offered solutions.

But they stayed.

In their presence, Maeve didn't have to explain herself or perform resilience. She didn't have to minimise her pain or prove her competence. She could simply exist — tired, grieving, human.

And that was when she understood something she had missed before: Connection is not the opposite of independence. It is the companion to it.

Letting herself be seen did not make her weaker. It made her real. Allowing someone to walk beside her did not erase the distance she had already travelled — it honoured it.

Djilba taught her that belonging does not require surrendering strength. It requires recognising that strength grows deeper when it is shared.

Maeve stopped asking herself the question she had carried for years: Can I do this alone?

Instead, she asked something gentler. Truer. Who walks with me?

And once she allowed herself to answer honestly, everything shifted.

Reflection — Djilba (Connection)

Djilba is the season of connection — of family, community, and the invisible threads that hold us upright when we are too tired to stand alone. It reminds us that growth is not sustained through isolation, but through relationship.

Maeve's story teaches us that companionship does not diminish resilience; it deepens it. True connection does not rescue us from our struggles or remove our pain. Instead, it reminds us that we were never meant to carry life unaided.

This week, notice who has walked beside you — not to fix you, but to remain with you. And if you are able, consider who you might walk alongside in return.

Belonging is not found in independence alone — it is found in allowing ourselves to be seen.

Belonging begins when we allow ourselves to be seen.

Week Forty-One

The Language of Staying...

Lucas had always been good with words.

He knew how to explain things clearly, how to soften hard truths, how to find the right phrase for most situations. Words had been his way of connecting — of making sense of the world and helping others make sense of it too.

But when life grew complicated, his words began to feel small.

It happened when a close friend lost her mother.

Lucas arrived at her door carrying all the things he thought she would need — carefully chosen sentences, reassurances about time and healing, gentle reminders that she wasn't alone. He had rehearsed them on the drive over, wanting desperately to say the right thing.

But the moment he stepped into her house, he felt it.

Grief has a weight that language cannot lift.

The room was quiet in a way that felt heavy, as though sound itself had slowed. His friend sat at the table; her hands wrapped around a mug she hadn't touched. Lucas opened his mouth — and stopped.

Nothing he had prepared belonged there.

So instead of speaking, he stayed.

He made tea. He washed dishes that didn't need washing. He listened when she spoke and didn't rush to fill the spaces when she didn't. He sat beside her through silences that stretched and sagged, resisting the urge to repair what could not be fixed.

And something unexpected happened.

The absence of words became the most honest language he had ever spoken.

In the days that followed, Lucas kept showing up. He checked in when others had returned to their routines. He remembered dates that carried quiet weight. He sent messages that didn't ask for replies — just reminders of presence.

Djilba taught him something he hadn't learned through language alone: connection is not built through eloquence or solutions. It is built through consistency. Through return. Through the simple, faithful act of staying.

He learned that care is often communicated not in grand gestures, but in repetition — in being there again, and again, and again.

And that love, in its truest form, rarely announces itself.

It sits down.

It waits.

It stays.

Reflection — Djilba (Connection)

Djilba shows us that connection is an act, not a performance. It is formed through presence rather than precision, through steadiness rather than spectacle.

Lucas's story reminds us that we do not need answers to offer comfort. What people often need most is not to be fixed, but to be accompanied. Staying — especially when there is nothing to say — is one of the deepest expressions of care.

This week, notice where presence might matter more than

explanation. Sometimes love is not spoken — it is lived, quietly, over time.

Sometimes love is simply the courage to remain.

Week Forty-Two

We Are Shaped By Who Holds Us…

Amara used to believe she had become who she was through effort alone.

She told herself she was self-made — that her strength had been carved through discipline, endurance, and the quiet determination to keep going when things were hard. She valued independence, admired resilience, and wore self-reliance like a badge of honour.

For a long time, she credited herself for surviving.

But as the years passed, she began to notice a pattern she could no longer ignore.

The moments she grew the most were not solitary. They were relational.

She thought back to a teacher who had seen something in her long before she could name it herself — who spoke encouragement when she was shrinking, who offered belief as though it were something to be shared rather than earned. She remembered a friend who had gently confronted her avoidance, refusing to let her hide behind competence when honesty was required. She remembered a partner who had sat with her fear without rushing it away, who listened without trying to fix her.

Those moments had shaped her more deeply than any solitary victory ever had.

Djilba revealed what she had once overlooked: we are not shaped only by what we survive, but by who stands beside us while we do.

Connection was not incidental to her growth — it was formative.

Amara began to understand that the people she allowed close did more than offer company. They influenced how she spoke to herself. How safe she felt in uncertainty. How gently — or harshly — she interpreted her own mistakes. Their voices slowly became woven into her inner world.

With that awareness came responsibility.

She became more intentional — not about perfection, but about proximity.

She paid attention to who she listened to when she was unsure. Who she leaned on when she felt small. Who she allowed to shape the tone of her inner voice. She noticed which connections left her feeling steadier, clearer, more aligned — and which ones left her doubting herself, bracing, shrinking.

Connection, she learned, is not neutral.

It either strengthens us or strains us. It either supports our becoming or quietly erodes it.

So Amara chose more carefully.

Not from fear. From wisdom.

Because she finally understood that who holds us, shapes us.

Reflection — Djilba (Connection)

Djilba is the season of relationship — of kinship, community, and the unseen bonds that influence us more than we realise. It teaches us that growth does not happen in isolation, but in the presence of others who reflect, challenge, and support us.

Amara's story reminds us that connection is not passive. The people we allow close help shape our beliefs, our healing, and our sense of self. Choosing our community is one of the most powerful acts of self-respect we can make.

This week, notice who influences your inner world. Ask yourself gently: Who helps me grow softer, braver, clearer? And who drains me without offering support?

We grow in the direction of those who surround us.

Week Forty-Three

The Ones Who Knew My Name...

Peter spent years chasing belonging.

He moved from room to room trying to find it — adjusting his tone, softening his opinions, learning which parts of himself to hide so that he might be easier to accept. He became skilled at reading others, sensing what was required of him, and offering just enough of himself to be welcomed.

But welcome, he learned, is not the same as being known.

He learned how to be agreeable. How to be useful. How to be present without being seen. And still, something inside him remained restless. No matter how full the room, he often felt invisible.

Over time, the effort grew exhausting.

Disappointment has a way of stripping pretence, and eventually Peter stopped trying so hard. Not out of bitterness — out of fatigue. And in the quiet that followed, something unexpected happened.

A few people remained.

They didn't need reminders of his story. They noticed when his voice softened. They recognised the difference between his silence and his peace. They asked questions without rushing him toward answers. They didn't require him to perform or explain who he was becoming.

They simply knew him.

Djilba taught Peter that belonging is not about being recognised — it is about being remembered. It is not about standing out — it is about being held in mind and heart, even when you are not in the room.

Real connection, he learned, does not ask you to shrink. It does not reward you for disappearing. It does not confuse approval with intimacy.

Once Peter stopped chasing inclusion, he found something quieter and far more sustaining.

A small circle. A steady presence. A place where his name carried meaning.

And in that space, he discovered something he had been searching for all along — not visibility, but grounding.

Reflection — Djilba (Connection)

Djilba teaches us that connection is not measured by numbers, visibility, or validation. It is measured by depth — by who remains when performance ends and pretence falls away.

Peter's story reminds us that true belonging does not require effort or explanation. It arises in spaces where we are known, where our presence is noticed, and where our absence would be felt.

This week, notice who remembers you — not just your achievements, but your rhythms, your silences, your becoming. Those are the connections that sustain us through every season.

Belonging begins where you are known.

Week Forty-Four

How Love Moves Through Us…

Elaine once believed love was something you received.

Something offered by the right person. Something earned, protected, or lost. She learned early to watch for it — to notice who gave it freely and who withheld it — and to measure her own worth by how much of it came her way.

But life reshaped that belief.

As the years passed, love showed up in unexpected places. In the relentless care of small children who needed her long before they understood gratitude. In the slow, tender responsibilities of aging parents. In friendships that required listening more than speaking. In moments of quiet service to strangers whose names she would never know.

Through it all, Elaine noticed something subtle but profound.

Love did not sit still. It moved.

When she allowed herself to give without keeping score,

love seemed to pass through her rather than drain her. It softened her edges. It widened her capacity. It did not leave her empty — it left her open.

Djilba taught her that connection is not possession. Love is not something we hold tightly in our hands. It is something we participate in — a current we step into when we choose care over withdrawal, generosity over fear.

The love Elaine offered returned — but rarely in the way she expected.

It came back as support when she was too tired to ask. As kindness from unlikely sources. As timing that arrived just when she needed it. As resilience she hadn't realised that she had been building all along.

She stopped asking, Will this be returned? She began trusting movement instead.

Love, she learned, does not always circle back to us directly — but it never disappears. It changes form. It finds pathways. It continues its work.

And in allowing it to move freely through her, Elaine discovered something steady and sustaining.

Love was not something she waited for anymore.

It was something she lived.

Reflection — Djilba (Connection)

Djilba reminds us that love is relational energy — it flows between us, shaping bonds, softening boundaries, and sustaining community. Connection deepens when we stop trying to contain love and instead allow it to circulate.

Elaine's story teaches us that love is not diminished by giving. When shared without demand or expectation, it strengthens both giver and receiver, often in ways we cannot immediately see.

This week, notice how love moves through your life — where it is offered, where it is received, and where it continues to flow quietly beneath the surface.

Love does not belong to us — it moves through us.

Djilba to Kambarang (Connection → Renewal)

Transition:

From the warmth of Djilba's connections, we move into the flowering fields of Kambarang - the season of renewal. Connection has nourished us, and now we are ready to bloom.

Kambarang offers the gift of fresh beginnings, reminding us that after every hardship, there is hope. Renewal is not about starting over completely, but about stepping forward with new life and fresh courage, ready to embrace what lies ahead.

KAMBARANG

(October - November)
The season of birth and the emergence of new life, with reptiles emerging from hibernation and many plants flowering…

RENEWAL

A time of fresh starts and new beginnings.

Introduction to Kambarang (Renewal)

Kambarang is the season of renewal - the time when the land blooms again after the cold and the heavy rains. It reminds us that every end is a new beginning, and every loss is an opportunity for growth. In Kambarang, we are invited to leave behind what no longer serves us, to clear the old and welcome the new. This is the season of hope, of fresh starts, and of trusting that the universe will always make way for what we need.

Week Forty-Five

Waiting in Line to Turn Back Time...

Harold had spent much of his seventy-three years looking backward. He thought of the chances he never took, the people he never told he loved, and the dreams he had tucked neatly away in the drawer of "someday." Now, with illness carving lines into his face and pain echoing through his body, he felt as though he was waiting in a line he would never reach the front of - a line to turn back time.

Hospitals smelled of disinfectant and endings. The machines beeped steadily beside him, a cruel reminder of how much life he had measured by clocks, deadlines, and routines. Regret was a heavy companion. He whispered often to himself: "If only I could go back. If only I had more time."

One morning, as he sat in the hospital garden, wrapped in a blanket, Harold noticed a young boy crouched nearby. The child was watching a caterpillar inch across a leaf. With fascination, the boy pointed and said, "He's going to be a butterfly soon."

Harold smiled weakly. "Maybe he won't make it," he murmured.

The boy shook his head with certainty. "Oh, he will. That's what they do. They always change." Then he ran off, leaving Harold with the thought hanging in the air like birdsong.

That night, Harold lay awake thinking about that caterpillar. Renewal, transformation - was it possible for him, even now? He couldn't undo the past. But perhaps he could still live what was left, not as regret, but as a chance to begin again.

The next morning, Harold picked up a pen. His hand trembled as he wrote the first of many letters - to his estranged daughter, to old friends, to people he had lost along the way. He wrote apologies, gratitude, and love. Each word felt like a breath of life returning. Some letters were answered; some were not. It didn't matter. What mattered was that he had spoken at last.

Harold began to notice things he had ignored for years: the warmth of the sun through the window, the kindness in a nurse's tired smile, and the sound of laughter echoing down a hallway. For the first time, he was not waiting to turn back time. He was living in it - fully, presently, gratefully.

When his final day arrived, Harold's daughter sat at his bedside, holding his hand. He whispered to her with a faint smile, "I didn't get to turn back time. But I learned something better. Renewal isn't about starting over - it's about beginning again, wherever you are."

And with those words, Harold exhaled into peace, leaving behind not a story of regret, but a story of courage, renewal, and love found just in time.

Reflection: Kambarang (Renewal)

Kambarang is the season of wildflowers, of new life bursting through the soil, of colour returning after long grey months. It reminds us that renewal is not bound by age, time, or circumstance. It can arrive late, quietly, even in the final chapters of a life - and it still matters.

Harold's story shows us that we cannot turn back time, but we can choose what we do with the moments left. Renewal begins the instant we shift from regret to presence, from silence to speaking, from waiting to living.

This week, ask yourself: What can I begin again today? However small, every new step is a bloom of renewal.

Renewal is not about turning back time - it is choosing to begin again, right where you are.

Week Forty-Six

The Courage to Begin Again…

Rowan had already lived several lives by the time he realised this one was asking something new of him.

He had been many things over the years — dependable, resilient, loyal. The one who stayed. The one who held things together when others fell apart. He had endured seasons where survival itself felt like an achievement, where simply getting through the day counted as success.

When things broke, he learned how to rebuild. When they broke again, he learned how to endure.

Endurance became his identity.

There was comfort in it — a strange safety in knowing how to suffer well. Hardship had rules. You tightened your grip. You lowered your expectations. You kept going. Rowan knew that terrain intimately.

But Kambarang did not ask him to endure. It asked him to begin.

And that frightened him more than any winter ever had.

Beginning again offered no instructions. No guarantees. No familiar weight to brace against. There were no maps for this season, no clear markers of progress. Only the unsettling sense that standing still was no longer an option.

At first, he tried to approach renewal the way he had approached survival — cautiously, defensively, prepared for disappointment. But something inside him resisted that posture.

It arrived quietly, like a shift in the wind.

A thought surfaced one morning as he stood outside, watching light touch the edges of things he had long overlooked: What if this time I try differently? Not harder. Not tougher. Just differently.

That question changed the way he moved through his days.

Rowan stopped recreating the life he already knew how to survive. He loosened his grip on routines that kept him functional but not alive. He began making room for things he had once dismissed as impractical or indulgent — rest without guilt, joy without justification, moments of wonder that did not need to lead anywhere useful.

He allowed himself to want things again. Not urgently. Not desperately. Just honestly.

Renewal did not arrive as certainty or confidence. It arrived tentatively. Like testing the soil with bare hands after a long frost. The ground was still cool. Still unfamiliar. But it was no longer frozen.

Each small step forward carried a quiet revelation: beginning again was not erasing the past. It was honouring it — by refusing to stay where it had ended.

Rowan understood then that survival had kept him alive — but choice was what would let him live.

And for the first time in a long while, the future did not feel threatening.

It felt open.

Reflection — Kambarang (Renewal)

Kambarang reminds us that renewal is not about forgetting what has been endured — it is about allowing life to move forward again. After long seasons of holding on, this phase invites us to loosen our grip and trust that new growth does not dishonour the past.

Rowan's story teaches us that beginning again does not require certainty, confidence, or a clear plan. It requires willingness — the courage to try differently, to step forward without knowing exactly how things will unfold. Growth resumes not when we feel ready, but when we allow ourselves to choose again.

Renewal begins the moment we stop surviving and start choosing again.

Week Forty-Seven

The Version I Chose to Become...

Sofia once believed becoming was something that happened automatically.

She assumed time would do the work for her — that if she endured enough, lived long enough, survived what life handed her, she would simply arrive as the person she was meant to be. She trusted that experience alone would shape her, mould her, and refine her.

But time, she learned, only reveals. It does not decide.

That realisation came quietly, after a season of loss that rearranged her life without spectacle. There was no single breaking point, no dramatic collapse. Just a slow, undeniable awareness that she could not return to who she had been — and did not yet recognise who she was becoming.

She found herself standing in a kind of stillness.

Not lost. Not found. Just unfinished.

For the first time, Sofia did not rush to fill the space. She didn't distract herself with productivity or reach for quick reinvention. Instead, she paused — and let the silence speak.

In that pause, she began asking herself questions she had avoided for years.

Who am I when no one is watching? What do I protect, even when it costs me comfort or approval? What kind of life do I want to participate in — not someday, but now?

The answers did not arrive neatly. They surfaced slowly, sometimes uncomfortably, asking her to release versions of herself that had been built to survive rather than to live.

Kambarang invited her into conscious renewal.

Not a reinvention. A refinement.

Sofia began shaping herself gently, one decision at a time. She chose honesty over harmony when the truth mattered. Presence over productivity when her body asked for rest. Alignment over approval, even when it meant standing alone in rooms she had once worked hard to belong in.

She stopped explaining herself unnecessarily. Stopped shrinking to keep peace. Stopped postponing her values for a more convenient future.

The changes were subtle — almost invisible from the outside — but they took root deeply. She felt less divided, less pulled in opposing directions. The effort it once took to hold herself together began to ease.

One day, without announcement, she realised something had shifted.

She no longer felt fragmented.

The woman she was becoming felt familiar — not because she had been there before, but because she had always been possible. Beneath the adaptations, the compromises, the years of endurance, she recognised herself.

And for the first time, becoming felt less like striving — and more like returning.

Reflection — Kambarang (Renewal)

Kambarang teaches us that renewal is conscious. It is not something that happens to us — it is something we participate in. This season asks us to move forward with intention, to choose who we are becoming rather than defaulting to who we have been.

Sofia's story reminds us that growth is not accidental. We shape ourselves through the choices we make when no one is applauding, when clarity feels incomplete, and when the path ahead is still forming. Renewal begins when we stop waiting for permission and start choosing ourselves with awareness and integrity.

Renewal is choosing yourself again — this time with awareness.

Week Forty-Eight

What Bloomed After the Fire...

Gregory did not trust hope anymore.

Not because he was cynical — but because he had learned how easily it could be taken. Life had burned through too many things he once believed were permanent: carefully laid plans, relationships he thought would last, and versions of the future he had built with certainty and care.

Each loss made him quieter. More cautious. He stopped reaching forward and focused instead on managing disappointment before it arrived. Expecting less felt safer than being hopeful and wrong.

Fire has a way of doing that.

It doesn't just destroy what is fragile — it teaches us what we can no longer afford to lose again.

But Kambarang does not demand trust immediately.

It begins with proof.

Gregory noticed it first in small, almost dismissible ways. A conversation that felt unexpectedly easy. A morning where the air carried something lighter than grief. A moment of laughter that came without effort — and without guilt.

It startled him.

Something had survived the fire.

Not everything. Not the life he once imagined. But enough.

As he paid closer attention, he realised what remained had been stripped of illusion. What endured was no longer propped up by hope alone — it was grounded. Honest. Resilient because it was real.

The fire had not ruined him. It had clarified him.

It burned away what was unsustainable — the expectations built on fear, the relationships that required self-erasure, the identities formed to please rather than to live truthfully. What remained was simpler, quieter, and far more solid than anything he had lost.

Gregory stopped measuring renewal by what returned.

He began recognising it in what grew.

The way he trusted his instincts again. The way he allowed joy without interrogating it. The way he stood more firmly in himself, no longer bracing for collapse at every good moment.

Renewal, he learned, does not mean nothing was lost.

It means something meaningful survived.

So he tended what was growing — gently, deliberately. He did not rush to rebuild a life that looked impressive. He cultivated one that felt honest. He protected what had proven it could endure.

And in doing so, Gregory discovered something he never expected: Hope did not betray him. It simply required different soil.

Reflection — Kambarang (Renewal)

Kambarang teaches us that renewal often follows destruction — not as replacement, but as transformation. What blooms after hardship is not a return to what was, but an emergence of what can now survive.

Gregory's story reminds us that loss does not erase meaning. Fire reveals what is essential. When we allow ourselves to tend what remains — rather than mourning what cannot return — renewal becomes possible, not because life is safe again, but because we are truer.

What blooms after the fire grows because it was real enough to survive it.

Week Forty-Nine

Learning to Receive…

Courtney was excellent at giving.

She anticipated needs before they were spoken. She remembered birthdays, carried emotional weight, showed up early, stayed late, and held space when others fell apart. Giving was instinctive — effortless, even. It was how she loved. How she proved her worth. How she stayed connected.

Receiving, however, was another matter entirely.

When care was offered to her, her body tightened. Compliments were brushed aside. Help was declined quickly, politely, almost reflexively. Rest felt indulgent. Dependence felt dangerous. Somewhere along the way, Courtney had learned that being needed was safer than needing.

Kambarang arrived quietly, as it often does.

Not with collapse — but with depletion.

After a long season of giving from empty hands, Courtney noticed the signs she had been ignoring. Fatigue that sleep didn't fix. Irritability where patience once lived. A subtle resentment toward the very people she loved most. She was still functioning — but she was no longer nourished.

Something had to change. Not her generosity. But the imbalance beneath it.

The first shift was uncomfortable. When someone asked how she was and waited for a real answer, she hesitated — then told the truth. When help was offered, she practised saying yes instead of explaining why she didn't deserve it. She let meals be made for her. Let others check in. Let herself rest without apologising for it.

It felt awkward. Exposing. Almost wrong.

But slowly, something softened.

Courtney realised that receiving did not erase her strength — it revealed another kind of it. The strength to trust. To be held without losing herself. To believe that care did not always come with conditions.

She stopped measuring her value by how much she could give before breaking.

She learned that renewal is not powered by effort alone. It requires nourishment — emotional, physical, relational. Growth needs both movement and stillness. Giving and receiving. Holding and being held.

Courtney did not become less generous. She became more whole.

And in allowing herself to receive, she discovered that love had far more room to move.

Reflection — Kambarang (Renewal)

Kambarang teaches us that renewal includes receptivity. Growth does not happen through effort alone — it requires nourishment, rest, and the courage to accept care without justification.

Courtney's story reminds us that giving and receiving are not opposites — they are partners. When we allow ourselves to receive what we once only gave, we create sustainability, balance, and deeper self-respect.

Renewal deepens when we allow ourselves to receive what we once only gave.

Week Fifty

The Life I Am Still Becoming…

Elias no longer believed life was meant to be finished.

There was a time when he chased completion — the sense that one day he would arrive. That the work would be done, the lessons mastered, the questions answered. He moved through life collecting milestones like proof: careers built, responsibilities met, and crises survived.

But each time he thought he had reached the place where everything would finally settle, life shifted again.

At first, this unsettled him. He wondered what he was doing wrong. Why contentment never stayed as long as he expected. Why clarity always seemed temporary.

Then Kambarang arrived and reframed everything.

As the land bloomed once more — not as it had before, but in its own renewed way — Elias saw the pattern he had been resisting. Renewal was not a reward at the end of endurance. It was part of the rhythm. A return, not to certainty, but to openness.

He realised he had been asking the wrong question.

Instead of Am I there yet? He began to ask, Am I still open?

Open to learning something new about himself. Open to changing his mind. Open to joy arriving in unfamiliar forms. Open to the possibility that life could keep expanding rather than narrowing with age.

This shift softened him.

He stopped judging himself for not having everything resolved. He released the pressure to be a finished product. He allowed himself to remain curious — about people, about purpose, about who he might still become.

There was relief in that.

Becoming, Elias learned, is not a task to complete. It is a relationship — with time, with experience, with the self that keeps unfolding.

Some seasons ask us to endure. Some ask us to rebuild. And some, like this one, simply ask us to stay receptive.

Elias no longer needed life to make sense all at once.

It was enough to keep participating.

Reflection — Kambarang (Renewal)

Kambarang reminds us that renewal is ongoing. Life does not ask us to arrive at a final version of ourselves — it asks us to remain willing, curious, and engaged with what is still unfolding. This week reflect upon, Where in my life am I still becoming — and am I willing to stay open to that unfolding?

Elias's story teaches us that growth does not end with age, experience, or understanding. Becoming is not something we finish; it is something we return to, again and again, with gentler expectations and deeper awareness.

Renewal is remembering that we are always still becoming.

Week Fifty-One

Hold On, Linda...

Linda was so tired.

Not the kind of tired sleep could fix, but the bone-deep exhaustion that comes from constantly having to explain yourself, soften yourself, shrink yourself. She had worked hard all her life. She showed up with kindness. She believed in positivity, in doing the right thing, in lifting others where she could. And still, she was treated like she didn't belong.

At work, her questions were met with irritation instead of answers. Her words were cut short with "leave it there." Conversations ended the moment she entered the room. She was described as having "poor communication" or "bad energy," when all she had done was speak honestly and differently.

Different became the label that followed her everywhere.
Let's put Linda over there.
Let's not talk about it.
Let's ignore it and move on.
Even silence can wound.

By the time her 54th birthday arrived, Linda felt invisible and unbearably exposed all at the same time. Her heart hurt in a way that had no language. Even her children, caught in their own pain, were angry — not understanding that their mother was drowning, not failing.

Linda reached a place beyond despair. Beyond hope. Beyond the belief that she mattered.

She didn't want to be here anymore.

What Linda couldn't see — because pain narrows our vision — was that she was never the problem. She was a light-bearer in places that thrived on shadows. A high-vibrational soul in environments that punished authenticity. People didn't reject her because she was wrong — they rejected her because her presence reflected what they were unwilling to face.

And then, something small happened. Not a miracle. Not a grand speech. Just a message. A simple, kind message from someone who truly saw her. "You matter. I see you. Please hold on."

It didn't erase the pain. It didn't fix everything. But it cracked the darkness just enough for light to slip through. Enough for Linda to pause. Enough to breathe. Enough to choose not to end her story — not today.

Linda didn't suddenly feel strong. She didn't feel healed. But she felt seen. And sometimes, that is enough. So Linda stayed. Not because everything was suddenly okay — but because renewal doesn't always arrive as rebirth. Sometimes it arrives as a whisper that says: Hold on. Just for now.

Reflection: Kambarang (Renewal)

Kambarang is the season of renewal — when life begins to stir again after long, cold months. It reminds us that renewal doesn't always mean blooming brightly. Sometimes it simply means choosing to stay.

Linda's story teaches us that being different is not a flaw — it is often a sign of light. And light is sometimes met with resistance in places not ready to receive it. When we are persecuted for our authenticity, it does not mean we are wrong — it means we are powerful.

If you are reading this and feel unseen, unheard, or pushed into the shadows, remember this: Your presence matters. Your light matters. And even the smallest kindness can change the course of a life — including your own.

Hold on. Just for now.

Renewal sometimes begins not with healing — but with choosing to stay.

Week Fifty-Two

Waiting for Karma in Pink Shoes...

Life is short. Lila had always known it, but it struck her most deeply when she lost a dear friend far too soon. She promised herself right there and then that she would never live life as a bitter person, never waste time clinging to those who drained her spirit, and never settle for less than a love built on respect and kindness.

Still, life hadn't always gone the way she had hoped it would. She had stumbled, made mistakes, hurt others at times, and carried regrets she couldn't erase. Yet every night she prayed for guidance, asking for the strength to grow into the woman she longed to be - a woman of kindness, faith, and resilience.

"I believe in karma," she often told herself. "What you give out is what comes back." So she gave freely - her time, her compassion, her smile. She poured herself into her work, teaching children to love stories the way she did, even when the days were long and the recognition was small. She gave more than she received, because she trusted that one day, in God's time, the blessings would circle back to her.

Sometimes it was hard. Watching others succeed while she waited tested her faith. But whenever doubt crept in, she reminded herself: Good things take time. And I will keep walking forward.

Her friends teased her about her favourite pink shoes - worn and scuffed, but always on her feet. To her, they were more than shoes. They were a symbol of her journey: bright, hopeful, and imperfect, but carrying her step by step toward the life she believed was waiting.

She imagined the day when her karma would catch up - when she would be that tenured teacher, shaping young minds with wisdom and joy. When her health would be strong, and her body alive with energy. When she would walk beside someone who loved her not for who she could become, but for who she already was.

Until then, she kept walking - one step, one prayer, one act of kindness at a time. She chose to live as though the life she dreamed of was already on its way.

Because she believed it was.

And perhaps that was the secret all along: karma wasn't something she had to wait for. It was something she created with every step she took in those pink shoes.

Reflection: Kambarang (Renewal)

Kambarang is the season of wildflowers and beginnings, a reminder that renewal comes not all at once but step by step. It invites us to trust that the seeds we plant in kindness and faith will bloom in their own time.

This story reminds us that while we may not always see the fruits of our goodness immediately, every step we take in integrity is shaping the life we long for. Renewal comes in trusting the timing, walking with hope, and creating the future with the choices we make today.

This week, take a moment to notice how far you've already walked. Even if your dreams feel distant, each step is a promise that renewal is already unfolding.

Renewal begins the moment we choose to walk in faith, trusting that life will bloom in its time.

Author's Note - From My Heart to Yours

As we journey through the seasons of life, we inevitably face moments of stillness, change, and challenge. The seasons - both of the earth and of the heart - offer us lessons that help us grow, adapt, and renew. We may find clarity in observation, strength in resilience, and peace in connection. And though each season may look different, they are all part of the same cycle.

Life doesn't promise smooth paths, but it does promise opportunities - opportunities to rise, to transform, to become who we are meant to be. Every step, whether small or great, moves us toward the person we are destined to become. Every hardship we endure is an invitation to learn, to reflect, and to renew our purpose.

No matter what season we are in, we are always becoming. Through each change, each loss, each new beginning, we are given the gift of growth. Like the seasons, we too can start again, shedding what no longer serves us and welcoming the fresh start that awaits.

In the end, we are never truly alone. As we connect with others, we are reminded of the power of love, compassion, and understanding. And through it all, we continue moving forward with courage, knowing that every season brings us closer to our true self - a self that is always ready to bloom again.

"Every season in life is an opportunity to grow, to change, and to reconnect with the light within us."

Acknowledgements

Thank you Marinda Carolyn x

Thank you Terry & Silla xx

...Sometimes there are truly no words big enough. Thank you for your unwavering support and encouragement in bringing this book to life...

About The Author

MAL STEVENS - THE AUTHOR was born in the small, country town of Geraldton, Western Australia, and at the very tender age of three - after discovering a love for reading whilst sitting at her Pops feet whilst he read in his library, decided that she would someday become an Author. Often her family and friends thought her weird because no matter where she was, she could always be found with her nose in a book…and if her nose wasn't in a book because of reading it, then it could be found in one of her many hundreds of journal notebooks filled with fanciful made-up stories, and vivid descriptions about her life in general, and poetry.

Today, I am a Registered Nurse by Trade, a Mum 24/7, a Mining and Construction Industry Site Medic by day, and a writer by night. I find writing very therapeutic, and I happily and passionately lose myself to it on a daily basis.

Shine, Shine, Shine.

With Lots of Love xxx

An Excerpt from 'Light Codes: The Art of Stillness'

in silentio invenies te ipsum

There's no single "right" amount of time - it depends on intention and consistency.

But here's what both modern neuroscience and ancient practice suggest:

Purpose	Optimum Duration	Frequency	Why it Works
Daily grounding / stress relief	10–15 minutes	1–2 times daily	Calms the nervous system, reduces cortisol, trains focus.
Deep emotional release / inner journey	20–30 minutes	A few times a week	Allows entry into theta brainwaves (deep healing state).
Spiritual growth / energy attunement	15–25 minutes	Daily	Enhances energy flow, awareness, and intuitive expansion.

The "Light Codes: The Art of Stillness" theme is perfect as it aligns beautifully with how long the mind needs to shift from beta (thinking) to alpha/theta (healing and creativity).

Consistency matters more than duration — 15 minutes daily is far more transformative than one long weekly session.

"You have never been lost. You were simply waiting to remember."

Preface

There is a language older than words—
the quiet pulse of the stars,
the breath between heartbeats,
the stillness that remembers where we came from.

You are a being of light, woven from the same essence as the constellations. Yet life on Earth can make even the brightest soul forget. The noise, the haste, the heaviness of modern living veil the truth that peace has never been lost—it has only been forgotten beneath layers of thought.

This little book is your map home.

Within these pages, you will find a simple, sacred practice—fifteen minutes a day that can open gateways of calm, clarity, and remembrance. Through meditation and the gentle currents of star being energy healing, you will learn to listen again—to your breath, to your energy, to the whisper of the stars within you.

Meditation transformed my life completely. It softened my fears, rekindled my intuition, and restored the quiet joy that waits beneath every storm. In stillness, I found the Universe breathing with me—guiding, healing, reminding.

You don't need a mountaintop or a monastery. You only need this moment, and a willingness to pause.

Meditation is not about becoming something new—it is about remembering who you already are.

It is natural, loving, and profoundly empowering. It is the pathway back to your own starlight.

May these words and practices be your lantern.

May you rediscover your own rhythm of peace.

And may your light ripple out into the world — one breath, one heartbeat, one star at a time.

With infinite love and luminous blessings,
Mal Stevens x

"In the stillness between breaths, the stars begin to whisper who you've always been."

Introduction

This little book is not only about learning how to meditate—it is about remembering how to be.

It is about quieting the noise long enough to hear your soul again.

You will, of course, learn the practical steps: how to meditate, when, where, and why.

But far more importantly, you will discover what meditation truly is—a sacred return to presence. A remembering of your connection to the greater whole: to the Earth beneath you, the breath within you, and the stars above that are made of the same light as your spirit.

When practiced with intention, meditation reshapes everything it touches.

It calms the mind, softens the heart, and reawakens the energy systems that nourish the body.

It can improve your physical health, deepen emotional balance, awaken intuition, and strengthen your connection to the Source of all life—whatever name you give it: Universe, Spirit, God, or simply Love.

Through stillness, people have found healing for anxiety and fear.

They have released old grief, rebalanced their hormones, soothed inflammation, restored focus, and rediscovered the joy they thought they'd lost.

Meditation is not magic—it is simply *you* returning to your natural state of harmony.

Many believe meditation is about emptying the mind or sitting perfectly still in the lotus pose, trying not to think. But true meditation is not about escaping thought; it is about observing it.

It is learning to watch the endless dance of the mind with compassion, until—like dust settling on sunlight—everything becomes clear again.

In these pages, you will come to understand the inner workings of your mind and energy field. You'll see how your thoughts shape your health, how your emotions guide your vibration, and how your spirit communicates through sensation and silence.

You will learn gentle, practical ways to still the "monkey mind," release tension, and open the sacred channels of peace, joy, and creativity that have always lived within you.

Each breath you take during meditation is a declaration of sovereignty.

A choice to step out of the noise and come home to yourself.

With time, you will find that the chatter fades, your intuition deepens, your energy brightens, and your heart expands to meet the rhythm of the stars once more.
It may sound miraculous, but it is not too good to be true. It is your birthright.

For too long, the simple truth has been hidden in plain sight—that stillness is the most powerful medicine we possess.

Now, both science and spirit agree: the light you seek has always been within you.

And all it asks for… is fifteen minutes a day.

"The stars have never been far away — they've only been waiting for your eyes to close and remember."

Cosmic Overload & the Quiet Within

In recent years, a growing body of clinical research has confirmed what seers and star-beings have known for ages: our modern lives carry a heavy load—not just of busyness, but of energetic turbulence, unprocessed emotion, and silent disconnection from the deeper currents of existence.

Meditation is no longer considered an obscure Eastern ritual—it has entered mainstream consciousness as a natural, simple and profoundly powerful healing practice.

As you read this book, you may already sense the call of something greater—a longing not just to relax, but to awaken. Whether you are new to meditation or have dipped your toes into its still waters before, this guide will help you step deeper: understanding what meditation truly is, how it can transform your entire life, and how you can easily make it a daily ritual of remembrance.

If you are committed to meditating properly, the first step is to recognise *why* it matters—not only for your physical or mental health, but for your spiritual alignment as a being of light and connection. Many people begin meditation simply because they wish to ease their overload, quiet their minds, or shift an inner frequency (personal growth).

But did you know that through regular meditation you can dramatically improve your well-being by clearing the subtle burdens your body and energy field carry? Research shows that meditation can reduce inflammation, modulate deep brain regions tied to emotional regulation and memory, and support the healing of your multi-dimensional self.

Our contemporary Western lives often carry a relentless sense of overload—and not just physical tasks. We juggle work, family, homes, social obligations—and underneath that, many of us bear the echoes of past trauma, unspoken fears, energetic imprints from another lifetime. In short: we carry layers of accumulated burden.

In the traditional "fight-or-flight" model the body cycles between beacon alerts and rest; but what we now face is often a state of "still threat"—not a lion in the bush, but a memory, an expectation, a ripple of energy signalling "You must act." The body responds. The mind responds. And yet no primal action is required—and still the energy circulates. We stay in high-alert modes much longer than nature ever intended.

Here's where star being energy healing and the meditation we'll practice together come in. Star being energy healing invites you to release not only the surface symptoms of overload, but the unseen: energetic blockages, subconscious beliefs, past-life echoes, the starlit imprint of your being that's been dimmed in earthly time.

Because when we dwell too long in the state of perceived urgency—when we live perpetually on the edge of our survival systems—our body cannot function as it was designed to: digestion slows, immunity weakens, creativity dulls, clarity clouds, sense of purpose dims. Research shows many of our common health issues—from anxiety and skin conditions to chronic fatigue and digestive disorders—are now linked with this prolonged state of overload.

But here's the luminous truth: You are not broken. You are recalibrating.

Your nervous system, your energy body, the star code within you—they all remember peace. Through meditation you are invited into stillness. You are called into presence.

You are returning to your own frequency of light.

Soon in this book you'll find a practical list of gentle daily practices that will significantly ease your overload and awaken your starlight.

You don't need to climb a mountain. You just need a breath, a quiet space, and fifteen minutes a day to reclaim the truth of your light-body.

"Every breath of stillness is a galaxy unfolding within you."

www.ingramcontent.com/pod-product-compliance
Lightning Source LLC
Chambersburg PA
CBHW022053290426
44109CB00014B/1080